# The Stairway of Freemasonry
## 30 Short Talks and Questions

# The Stairway of Freemasonry
## 30 Short Talks and Questions

**Julian Rees**

Lewis Masonic

*Front cover:* Stairway in Bruchsal Castle, Germany, built 1722-1733, the residence of Prince-Bishop Damien Hugo von Schoenborn. Architect: Balthasar Neumann. *AKG Images*

First published 2007

ISBN (10) 0 85318 2728
ISBN (13) 978 0 85318 2726

Published by Lewis Masonic

An imprint of Ian Allan Publishing Ltd, Hersham, Surrey KT12 4RG.
Printed in England by Ian Allan Printing Ltd, Hersham, Surrey KT12 4RG.

Visit the Lewis Masonic website at www.lewismasonic.com

# Contents

## Darkness and Light

## The Centre

# Preface

For any enquiring mind, whether Freemason or not, this little book sets out to help answer questions – not so much: 'What does it mean?' but rather: 'What can it mean?', since the journey is concerned not with learning other people's answers, but in working out answers for yourself.

If you are not a Freemason, you may want answers to questions such as the following:
- Why can I not become a Freemason by reading about it in a book?
- What would initiation do for me?
- What is the point of secrets in Freemasonry?
- Why are the square and compasses in Freemasonry such a universal symbol?
- What are Masonic symbols for? Do they mean anything?
- Can Freemasonry be as meaningful for me as my religion?
- By being a Freemason, can I be closer to God?

If you are already a Freemason, you may want answers to other, but similar questions:
- Why are we called Free Masons?
- If secrets in Freemasonry are not to hide something, what are they for?
- What does the ritual mean when it talks of avoiding fear and rashness?
- How can symbols best be used?
- Can working tools really be used to make me a better person? If so, how?
- Why is it said that lodges stand on holy ground?
- How am I to understand light in a symbolic sense?

The list is almost endless! And the great thing is that you can devise your own questions, and then, by contemplation, provide the answers to them, or work out the answers in a group. But don't expect all members of the group to agree. We all have our own interpretation of Masonic symbols and practices, and there is no dogma, no 'right' answer.

This book has been conceived as a companion volume to its earlier partner *Making Light*. Unlike that book, however, these essays can be read aloud in open lodge as well as being studied on your own at home. Some of the essays overlap each other, underlining the importance of central themes in different parts of the ritual. They are designed so that they can be used as oral instruction for an aspirant or more widely in the lodge. Incorporated in each of them are some thoughts or propositions – responding to these gives an opportunity for your own input. Writing about a half-page is suggested. You need not limit yourself to a half-page. You need not write as much as a half-page. You need not write anything at all. Your progress is entirely up to you: how much, how little, and at what speed. Above all, enjoy the journey.

# THRESHOLDS

## 1 Gateway to Celestial Realms

*How to climb*

'As Jacob journeyed towards Padan-aram in the land of Mesopotamia, being weary and benighted on a desert plain, he lay down to rest, taking the earth for his bed, a stone for his pillow, and the canopy of heaven for a covering. He there in a vision saw a ladder, the top of which reached to the heavens, and the angels of the Lord ascending and descending thereon.'

*Part of the first lecture*

There are a few legends from the Judaeo-Christian Bible in Masonic ritual, of which by far the most important is that describing Jacob's ladder. This is the story in the Book of Genesis which tells of Jacob's vision.

In the legend, Jacob went out from Beersheba and went towards Haran. He came to a certain place and stayed there all night, because the sun had set. He took stones and laid them as pillows, and lay down to sleep. As he slept he dreamed, and in his dream he saw a ladder set up on the earth, the top of it reaching to heaven, and the angels of God ascending and descending on it. God stood above it, and said, 'I will give to you the land on which you lie, to you and to your seed; and in your seed shall all the families of the earth be blessed. And behold, I am with you, and will keep you wherever you go.'

Jacob awoke out of his sleep, and said, 'Surely the Lord is in this place, and I knew it not.' And he was afraid, and said, 'How dreadful is this place! This is none other but the house of God, and this is the gate of heaven.' And he rose up early in the morning, and took the stone that he had put for his pillows, and set it up for a pillar, and poured oil upon the top of it, after which he made a vow, saying, 'If God will be with me, and will keep me in this way that I go, and will give me bread to eat, and raiment to put on; then shall the Lord be my God. And this stone, which I have set for a pillar, shall be God's house.'

As with all legends, we have no way of ascertaining its factual truth. In effect, it is an allegory, since its lesson is one which is depicted for us in such a way that it is we who discern what the meaning is, and we who profit by the lesson it contains but does not immediately reveal.

Jacob was fleeing from his brother, whom he had wronged. God nevertheless saw the good in Jacob, and wanted to demonstrate to him that, despite the fact that he had done wrong, he was capable of greatness, if he would own God and stay with him. To do so, he showed Jacob not only the route to the celestial realms, the ladder, but that this ladder was a two-way conduit, angels ascending to God taking our petitions to Him, and angels descending to earth, bringing divine providence. It was thus the connection between earth and heaven, demonstrating that which for Freemasons is of the utmost importance: that man and God can be one, God representing the macro part of the universe, and man being the mirror-image, the micro counterpart.

There is another Masonic symbol which demonstrates the same aspect of our union with God, and that is the hexalpha, or six-pointed star, otherwise known as Solomon's seal. This figure is formed by inverting one triangle on top of another, so that the angle of one points to heaven, the other to earth, and these triangles, being interlaced, demonstrate the one-ness of God and man. It is thus an expression of heaven and its reflection on earth, the divine and its reflection in creation, the connection between spirit and matter.

King Solomon, whose seal this originally was, established Jerusalem as the city of justice and peace. He is said to have been given both wisdom and knowledge. Another part of the lecture, speaking about the three great pillars supporting a Freemason's lodge, names those pillars as wisdom, strength and beauty. Of these, the Ionic pillar, wisdom, is said to represent King Solomon

> ....for his wisdom in building, completing and dedicating the Temple at Jerusalem to God's service...

and so we have another allegory, that of the building of a temple.

Of all the thresholds in Freemasonry, this one is the most potent. The allegories we have investigated here are those of salvation after transgression, of the route from earth to heaven, of man and the temporal world being a reflection, a mirror-image of heaven. We sense the one-ness of God and man, of the importance of wisdom and knowledge, and of the promise that we too can erect and maintain a temple, the temple of moral truth and virtue, in ourselves in the first place, and in concert with our Brethren, a temple to humanity in the wider world.

**To explore:**

• Acknowledging God's power in us
• The way back after wrongdoing
• Allegory of angels ascending, descending
• Connections, conduits, between God and man
• Macro universe, micro universe
• Godliness in man
• The hexalpha and the ladder
• Building a personal temple to morality
• Building a general temple to morality

# 2 Preparation

*Freedom to serve*

'The Brethren from the north, east, south and west will take notice that Mr Smith is about to pass in view before them, to show that he is the candidate, properly prepared, and a fit and proper person to be made a Mason.'
*Announcement before the aspirant's pilgrimage in the first degree*

This is the first instance, in initiation, that the aspirant and all the Brethren of the lodge interact. It is a ritualised way of the Brethren taking a close look at the man who is presenting himself for initiation, although he may have been interviewed by some of the Brethren beforehand.

But it *is* a ritualised procedure – the members of the lodge will learn very little on a tour of inspection of this kind. The point of this procedure is, as with all Masonic allegories, that it is subject to ritualisation. We 'go through the motions', and therein lies its importance. It is there to remind us of the underlying importance of getting to know and uniting with the aspirant. 'From the north, east, south and west', in other words all the Brethren, joined together in support of the aspirant in his endeavour. The force of ritual, and the repetition of ritual, is to free the aspirant from distraction, thereby focusing the mind on one particular theme, to help him to hear the single note being played, and to harmonise himself with the allegory, so that he may understand its power for good.

In some Masonic jurisdictions, as the aspirant approaches the east, the Brethren rattle their swords. The noise increases as he approaches the east, and dies away as he returns to the west. This is a warning to the aspirant, that he should not approach the mysteries in a flippant manner, but take his new profession seriously. Although he is blindfolded, he can sense that the place where the noise is loudest, the east, is an important place to be.

'Properly prepared'. The aspirant may like to look at this preparation on two distinct levels. First, it is obvious that he has been physically prepared in a very particular way. That preparation is one which will disorient him and confuse him physically – a disengaging of his outward faculties to enable his inner contemplation to takeover. The inner preparation should be within his own heart. We read later on:

'Where were you first prepared to be made a Mason?'

'In my heart.'

So the relevant preparation takes place at a deeper level. Freemasonry is not an academic pursuit. In the second degree we speak about contemplating the intellectual faculty, but this does not refer to the intellect of the mind, rather the intellect of the heart. Here, feelings and intuition are important. To activate these feelings, these insights, the aspirant needs a heart that is free, and an important part of preparation will be for the aspirant to free himself from material concerns, emotional burdens and other aspects that may weigh heavily on him, to ensure that he approaches Freemasonry with an open heart.

In Freemasonry we have allegories of the removal of freedom from the aspirant. We remove his freedom so that he can, later, attain to a greater freedom still. In the same way

> **To explore:**
>
> • Ideas of presenting yourself for inspection
> • Initiation – an individual aspiration? A group aspiration?
> • Value of ritualised behaviour – preparing by going through the motions
> • Value of ritual in enabling us to focus our mind
> • Freedom and servitude
> • Material freedom, spiritual freedom
> • Inner preparation
> • What the heart is for

13

that we need air to breathe, we need freedom. Freedom, which is not the same as licence, exists for Free Masons on a number of different levels. It may be freedom of conscience, freedom of thought and speech, freedom from ideological or political coercion, freedom from dogma, freedom to act in a positive way. The list is long. But here, the aspirant appears to have lost his freedom, to have arrived at a state of servitude, to be, in feudal terms, a bond man, and this is intentional. In a state of servitude, the aspirant is now prepared to be of service to his Brethren, his lodge and, beyond that, to be of service to mankind in general. The lesson here may be that he can attain freedom by being of service to others, since now he will serve, not out of compulsion, but of his own free will and agreement.

# 3 Groundwork

*Laying out the implements*

'Where were you first prepared to be made a Mason?'
'In my heart.'
'Where next?'
'In a convenient room adjoining the lodge.'
'Describe the mode of your preparation.'

*Questions to the aspirant in the first degree*

Preparation. Apart from the first question, these appear to refer to preparation on the most superficial level. Yet we might well consider that they represent preparation due to be made elsewhere, and in another fashion entirely. After all, allegories do not *describe* what is going on. They only *indicate* what might happen.

Preparation is important in many aspects of our everyday life. When we go to bed at night, we don't simply get into bed without first preparing ourselves, not only physically, but also mentally, for going to sleep. We let the level of energy die away so that we can feel relaxed enough to sleep. And when we get up in the morning, we make the bed with care and attention, so that the result is a neat one, not hurried or muddled. The Japanese way of making tea is a ceremony, a ritual in itself, demanding care and quietness. The host may spend several days going over the details so that his tea ceremony will be perfect. In a film recently a butler is seen laying down the cutlery on the table thoughtfully and carefully, checking that it is all the same distance from the edge, making the table look neat, and pleasing to the eye.

In today's world, much of such behaviour is labelled obsessive or compulsive, lacking in spontaneous fun or imagination. In that culture, wine is there to be drunk, not to be tasted with care and appreciated over time, allowing all its subtleties to become apparent as we go on the journey of experience.

So let us see Freemasonry as such a journey requiring care and attention, an antidote to the frantic pace of life outside the walls of the temple, as a part of the closing of the lodge in one working tells us:

> 'Brethren, you are now about to quit this safe retreat of peace and friendship, and mix again with the busy world; amidst all its care and employments, forget not those sacred duties which have been so frequently inculcated and recommended in this lodge. Be therefore discreet, prudent and temperate…'

Our approach to any Masonic work, in whichever degree, might therefore require such preparation as to 'put us in the right frame of mind', to help us relax, yet to be alert to the demands of the Masonic work we are about to undertake. As an example, after the Entered Apprentice has made his vow, the Master asks him

'Having been kept for a considerable time in a state of darkness, what in your present situation is the predominant wish of your heart?'

Consider for a moment that the Master may not be referring simply to the period of time that the aspirant has been blindfolded, but rather that he may have been, spiritually, in a state of darkness for a greater part of his life. The aspirant may have spent a considerable time preparing himself for this moment.

In another working, before the ceremony of initiation proceeds, the aspirant is led to a chamber of reflection, which is darkened. This chamber is furnished only with a table and chair, a skull, an hour-glass, a lit candle, a bell and writing materials with which he will give written answers to the following questions:

> **To explore:**
>
> • Care and attention in preparation
> • Aspects of inner preparation
> • Drinking wine, tasting wine
> • Experience as a journey
> • The contrast inside the temple and outside
> • Being in 'the right frame of mind'
> • Expressing feelings
> • Discretion, prudence and temperance

1. What is the destiny of mankind?
2. What do you expect of the Brotherhood for your spirit, your heart and your earthly happiness?
3. What can the Brotherhood expect of you?

At a certain level, such a preparation gives the aspirant the chance to express his feelings on these matters, feelings which may have been developing in himself over many years. He may never, in the outside world, have had the opportunity to express them or even to examine them himself to sense the importance they may have for him in life. For such an aspirant, the journey has truly begun.

# 4 Wages
## *Third degree audiences only*

*Debts paid, credits collected*

'Where did our ancient Brethren go to receive their wages?'
'Into the Middle Chamber of King Solomon's Temple.'
'How did they receive them?'
'Without scruple or diffidence.'
'Why in this peculiar manner?'
'Without scruple, well knowing they were justly entitled to them, and without diffidence from the great reliance they placed on the integrity of their employers.'

*Questions of the second degree*

Our degrees are delimited by thresholds. The important first degree threshold is crossed when the aspirant enters the temple. On passing that threshold he leaves behind him his previous attachment to material pursuits as he embarks on the journey leading him on to moral progress, and ultimately to God.

The second degree contains many useful lessons, distinguished by not one, but two thresholds. The aspirant arrives at the porchway, the access to the winding staircase. But he cannot yet ascend. His ascent is 'opposed' or, more correctly, checked by the Junior Warden, the guardian of the staircase, who needs to be assured that the aspirant is qualified to ascend; in other words that he has made sufficient progress in his moral pursuits to ascend to the next stage, a stage of more importance and significance. The proofs the Junior Warden needs are that the aspirant has made enough progress in his building in the first degree, and that he possesses the certificate gained as a result of that progress, namely the password leading to the next degree. As with so much else in Freemasonry, this is an allegory of his fitness, spiritually and morally, to proceed.

Now he is able to ascend the winding staircase, but this will take more time than the words of the ritual suggest. This staircase is an allegory of spiritual and intellectual advancement, and requires an acquaintance with the qualities of the five noble orders of architecture, as well as a good knowledge of how the seven liberal arts and sciences relate to life. Developing this will enable him to become more complete in himself.

At the top of the staircase, the aspirant then enters the middle chamber, having passed the second threshold, which he does by proving to the Senior Warden that he is a duly and truly qualified second degree Freemason, a Fellow of the Craft. We speak of him here receiving his wages, but in fact the channel of communication is two way – he goes into the middle chamber to receive what is due to him for his labour, but to earn that he must first pay off old debts, put right some old wrongs. In both the first and second degrees the aspirant has debts to pay. He uses his time as an Entered Apprentice freeing himself from material pursuits, passions and unworthy traits in his character. In the first degree the aspirant may have to forfeit aspects of his former life in order to reach enlightenment and develop his moral Self. He has to divest himself, symbolically, of worldly goods.

Now is the time to atone, so that he can then receive the second degree wages that are due to him, and gains of this kind must be accompanied by the settling of old debts to make them worthwhile. The great reliance which the aspirant must place on the integrity of his Employer is his appreciation, his insight, that spiritual benefits will flow from this. He now comes to know the name of God.

In the third degree, the aspirant once again stands in a porchway, but this time it is on the level above, namely that porch leading from the middle chamber to the sanctum sanctorum, emblematic of his impending union with God. In this holy of holies, he will find himself face to face with God, and begin to understand his own divinity. If we think of it in terms of milestones, his passage through the door of the temple in the first degree started his progress away from selfish impulses; his passage through the porchway in the second degree and through the doorway of the middle chamber enable him to acknowledge and settle up both his debts and credits, so that in the third degree he is able, unencumbered by material or selfish concerns, to know God.

---

**To explore:**

• Thresholds leading from, leading to
• Checking progress
• Second degree working tools in relation to progress
• The seven liberal arts and sciences
• Transgressions to be paid for
• Paying debts – receiving wages
• In the presence of God
• God without, God within

---

# 5 Entering the Holy of Holies
## *Third degree audiences only*

*The supreme threshold*

'Brother Smith, who has been regularly initiated into Freemasonry, passed to the degree of a Fellow Craft, and has made such further progress as he hopes will entitle him to be raised to the sublime degree of a Master Mason.'
'How does he hope to obtain the privileges of the third degree?'
'By the help of God, the united aid of the square and compasses, and the benefit of a password.'

*Exchange at the door of the temple in the third degree*

Freemasonry is a progressive science. In the second and third degrees, when we re-enter the temple after entrusting, we are invited by the Deacon to 'advance as a Mason' and 'advance as a Fellow Craft'. Each time we enter the temple, but especially at the start of our initiation, we are on a threshold, a threshold on to which, and from which, we advance into the next stage, advancing from darkness to light, from unknowing to knowing, from one qualification on to the next journey and, in the case of the third degree, from light back into darkness. But these are all thresholds, turning points, new beginnings.

There are other turning points, thresholds, within the degree ceremonies, changes of tone which serve to call our attention to a different direction, a different emphasis. One of these has been lost in English Freemasonry, although in other jurisdictions it is still in use – the chamber of reflection. The aspirant is shut away in a darkened room, on his own, surrounded by emblems of mortality – a skull, an hour-glass, a lit candle – to contemplate, for a considerable period of time, a number of questions. These include his own destiny and that of humankind, his reasons for wanting to be a Freemason, what he expects from Freemasonry and what Freemasonry can expect of him.

The aspirant arrives at another threshold in the first degree when he is led to the Master's pedestal. From this point on, there is no turning back without loss of honour. Now, by his vow, he will obligate himself in a bond more indissoluble than any he will ever again take in his life. The die is cast.

We are admitted to a second degree lodge 'by the help of God and the assistance of the square', a threshold characterised by the union of two powers – the power of God on the one hand, and on the other hand the power of the square, the foremost symbol in all of Freemasonry. The first of the three great lights is the Volume of the Sacred Law, God's revealed word to humankind; the second is the square, so at this point in the second degree, two of those great lights, no longer far-off symbols on the Master's pedestal, are given into our hands as emblems with which our journey may be advanced.

Once more, we pass the threshold of the vow, this time admitting us to participation in the privileges of the second degree, and this is in fact two thresholds. First, as the tracing board later tells us, the aspirant has to prove himself, at the porchway or entrance on the south side of the temple, to the Junior Warden, to whom he must give the password; in other words to make the transition from the first to the second degree. The second threshold comes at the top of the winding staircase, where the aspirant must prove himself to the Senior Warden once the sign, token and word of the second degree have been communicated to him. We may have noted, in passing, that at the pedestal the compasses had begun to emerge from behind the square.

So it is, in the third degree, that we are admitted 'by the help of God and *the united aid* of the square and compasses'. The square then will no longer predominate over the compasses – our material concerns will no longer take precedence over our spiritual progress, represented by the compasses, and thus all three of the great lights will be accessible.

We may believe then to have passed the last threshold, but this is not the case – there are still more to come in this sublime degree. We pass the threshold of the grave, leaving our own mortal nature with all its transgressions behind. We pass the threshold of the communication of the five points of fellowship, a sublime lesson of how to lead our lives in relation to humankind and our Brethren in particular. But of supreme importance, we pass from the middle chamber of the temple, where we become acquainted with the name of God, into the sanctum sanctorum, where the light of the blazing star floods in through the dormer, where we stand

> **To explore:**
>
> • Thresholds – going to, coming from
> • Advancement – material, spiritual
> • Reflection and contemplation
> • An indissoluble bond
> • Great lights – great powers
> • Symbolism of passing over the grave
> • One-ness of God and man
> • The blazing star

face to face with the Most High, and acknowledge our one-ness with divinity, and discover, finally, that which we sought to unfold by the prayer in the first degree, namely our own centre, our vital and immortal principle, the spark of divinity within ourselves.

# CONSTANCY

## 6 Fear, Rashness, Obedience

*Loss and gain*

'Do you declare that, avoiding fear on the one hand, and rashness on the other, you will steadily persevere… and afterwards act and abide by the ancient usages and established customs of the Order?'

*Before the aspirant approaches the Master's pedestal in the first degree*

It is important for the aspirant to understand two aspects of his physical condition on entering the temple. There is a cable-tow around his neck, by which he is figuratively being led forward. A dagger is presented to his heart. The one therefore would symbolically urge him forward, if he holds back; the other would resist him, if he attempts to rush forward.

Reticence and impetuosity, two opposed characteristics, neither of which, you might think, should have any part in progress. The aspirant has placed his trust in the Brethren, and it is they who will determine the pace of his progress, not he. This is a part of the humility we often speak of in Freemasonry.

But there is another, more telling aspect. Later in the ceremony, the aspirant is instructed in the first of the three working tools, the twenty-four inch gauge 'to measure our work by'. His progress ought perhaps to be a measured progress. He ought not to move forward impetuously, since steps in life accomplished in a considered way will achieve more. 'Don't rush into anything,' we are often warned. But perseverance is the flip side of that coin. Once having embarked on something, and once the aspirant has made a decision to move forward, he ought to see it through, and when that chosen course doesn't always run smoothly, then he will need the virtue of perseverance to see it through, even in the face of adversity and contrary influences.

Then the aspirant is being asked to abide by the laws and regulations of Freemasonry. This too is important. Think of a chain, the links of which are equal in shape and size. If one of those links were able to break loose and obey its own whims and desires, the chain itself would be useless; the whole depends upon the integrity of each member. Each link has not only the same purpose as the others, but also the same intent. This is not to say that we give up our individuality – far from it. The process of becoming a Freemason enhances our individuality, since we have now been removed from the bedrock of the quarry, and have become our own rough ashlar. But what the aspirant obligates himself to here is uniting with the Brethren, so that his own talents and his own skills are placed at the service of humankind, and to do so he adheres to the conduct and behaviour of the lodge, and through that to Freemasonry worldwide.

It has been said that 'Wisdom isn't valued much in today's world.' If you offer a teenager the choice between being famous and being wise, there is often not much of a contest. We may be afraid of wisdom because we are afraid of authority. Socrates defined prudence as practical wisdom, or knowledge of how to live, informing our reason. A child doesn't know that it is dangerous to cross a busy road until he is taught this by

> **To explore:**
>
> • Fear of doing something
> • Fear of not doing something
> • Danger in relation to gain
> • Perseverance and its relation to humility
> • Obedience and its relation to freedom
> • Balance between impulsiveness and reticence
> • Wisdom and prudence
> • Trust

those who do know. The aspirant seeking initiation into Freemasonry, having left the outside world, is in much the same helpless state and it is the task of the Master and Brethren to help him achieve the state of knowing, of wisdom.

Prudence here is important, and is one of the four cardinal virtues spoken of in the First Lecture. It is the moderating force between courage, which is generally a positive characteristic, and rashness, generally held to be negative. Hence we do not give an aspirant free rein the moment he enters the temple. We ask him, as a parent asks their child, to put his trust in us. This is not to say that we treat the aspirant as a child; merely that he places his trust in us in the same way. So the poignard will curb his rashness, but the cable-tow will lead him gently on, and encourage him to overcome his reticence and apprehension. The balance here is an important lesson, and will teach the aspirant that steady perseverance is the best course, now in the ceremony, and later in life.

# 7 Inducements, Incentives, Bias and Prejudice

## Motives for becoming a Freemason

After the Senior Warden presents the aspirant as properly prepared, the Master asks him if he is unbiased by the improper solicitation of friends against his own inclination, and uninfluenced by mercenary or other unworthy motive; if he has a good opinion of Freemasonry; if he seeks knowledge and wishes to serve his fellow-men.

'Unbiased by the improper solicitation of friends against your own inclination.' In a sense, we are back with freedom. Bias is 'to swerve from the right line', so we can assume that the aspirant's own inclination may well be such a right line, what we call obeying his instincts. He must be willing to proceed to initiation, to have a free will to travel the path because it is his own inclination, not because others want him to, for whatever reason. He can be figuratively blown off course when something is suggested to him, and he accepts it as a good idea without thinking. He may think this is a good path to follow, because his friends say it is, but he should be sure in his own heart that it is right for *him*. For instance, a simple desire for comradeship, although not a bad thing in itself, is not enough.

The next question, concerning mercenary motives, refers the aspirant again to the need to free himself from ideas of material advantage. Not only this, but he may even regard Masonic membership as in some way a route to career improvement or, still worse, self-aggrandisement. This touches on the important difference between self-centredness, which is egotistical, and being centred on himself, which may be the beginning of the journey to self-awareness and thus, eventually, to self-knowledge.

All of this, summed up, may be expressed in one question: 'What do you want from Freemasonry?' The Brethren want to know why the aspirant wants to join, but the Master is also reminding him that it is a question he should ask of himself, since before he goes any further, he must be clear about why he is joining.

Allied to this, of course, is: what does the aspirant think of Freemasonry? Is it all a game; is he joining out of mere curiosity; or does he really understand the quality of the organisation, a quality which he admires, and wishes to be united with? If so, then he will soon learn that Freemasonry is first and foremost about the pursuit of self-knowledge, and so that is a cause he will naturally wish to espouse and to follow, to make of it his own personal pursuit.

So it is important that the aspirant has a good opinion of Freemasonry, that he regards Freemasonry in the *right* way, as a quality that will free, enrich and enlighten him, and not only as a social grouping or a charitable organisation. He should certainly not have an opinion of Freemasonry based on some expectation of social or career advancement. He must want to seek knowledge, first of himself, and, through that, knowledge of the world around him and therefore of his fellow-men.

This last knowledge is important too, for by knowing his fellow-men he will the better be able to serve them. There is a paradox here – the aspirant seeks to underline the fact that he is free, but is being required to follow a path of servitude. In feudal times, and since then also, freedom was regarded as the opposite of servitude. Here, the aspirant is being asked to regard servitude as the freedom from himself, in order to serve others. Here, as so often in Freemasonry, a shift of perception is required.

Self-knowledge, and service to your fellow-men: how are these two linked? Pythagoras once said 'Man, know thyself; then thou shalt know the universe and God.' Implicit in this saying is the idea that,

> **To explore:**
>
> • Your own ideas of bias, instincts and a straight line
> • Being swayed, being true
> • What you want from Freemasonry
> • What you can give to Freemasonry
> • Your own ideas concerning self-awareness and self-knowledge
> • The value of self-knowledge
> • Some aspects of selflessness
> • Service to others

in order to know and understand others, the aspirant must first know himself. Understanding others, not having prejudices or erroneous views of them, is the first step towards being of service to them; hence if the aspirant progresses towards self-knowledge and self-awareness, he progresses equally towards harmony with, and support for, his fellow-men.

# 8 Obligation to Faithfulness

*A vow*

'Are you therefore willing to take a solemn obligation, founded on the principles I have stated, to keep inviolate the secrets and mysteries of the Order?'

*The Master to the aspirant before the latter makes his vow in the first degree*

All solemn undertakings are preceded by a vow, an undertaking. Too often in modern life, we will hear it said 'yes, don't worry, I'll do it' only to be disappointed later to find that it has not been done. And it is so easy to say. We may well have the best intentions – sincerely mean to do it, but become overtaken by events.

Initiation in many ancient rites required a solemn vow, as a way of underlining the importance and seriousness of the step. Another word for vow is obligation – an obligation to hold ourselves to a high standard of truthfulness at all times, and not to deviate from those things that we commit ourselves to.

All initiations are associated with the idea of a rite of passage, a transition from one state to another. Rites of passage are associated with childbirth, baptism, start of school, puberty, coming of age, graduation and weddings amongst other milestones in life. Masonic initiation is such a milestone. This transition marks a change in the status of a person, and has three stages – separation, liminality and incorporation.

So, in the first stage of initiation, we become separated from our old life and behaviour. We are blindfolded and have temporarily lost our freedom, in order to gain, later, a greater freedom. We are now in a 'betwixt and between' stage, neither completely separated, nor completely incorporated in the body of Freemasonry. This is the stage of liminality (Latin *limen*, a threshold). One's sense of identity dissolves, to some extent, bringing about disorientation. This stage is characterised by openness and indeterminacy and in this stage limits to thought, self-understanding and behaviour are relaxed, opening the way to something new.

In order to pass from this stage and become incorporated, we must swear a vow, an oath, an obligation to bind ourselves to our new state and association. If the goal of our Masonic path were not a supremely important one, a solemn vow would not be necessary, so the fact that such solemnity surrounds the aspirant's undertaking warns him, raises his level of anticipation, that the path he will tread is a very important one indeed. A trivial or flippant undertaking here simply will not do.

At the start of this oath of fidelity, this vow, the aspirant solemnly promises, in the presence of the Great Architect of the Universe, that he will always conceal and never reveal any of the secrets or mysteries belonging to Freemasons. Over centuries, detractors of Freemasonry have claimed this promise implies that there is something sinister or even illegal which Freemasons seek to conceal. The truth is something much less sensational. The power and value of a secret has a lot to do with who knows it, and how they use it. A secret is a currency whose value we need to learn. Freemasons bind themselves not to speak about how they become initiated, not because others must never know that secret, but because they should only come to know it if they are to be initiated – it is a secret that needs to be *experienced* not merely read about.

Initiation is much like creativity. If a composer is writing an opera, he doesn't perform parts of it before it is finished – a painter will not show his painting before he is ready. To do so would be to pour away all the creativity that he has so far put into it – the energy would be dissipated. Masonic initiation works best when the energy is in full flow, when the tension is at its highest.

Earlier we used the word fidelity. We would all agree that, if we are to bind ourselves to a brotherhood, an important part of that trust is to keep faith with our new Brothers. The sharing of the knowledge which will lead to self-knowledge must be something we restrict to those already initiated, otherwise the very term brotherhood ceases to have meaning.

So it is also that the aspirant pledges not to write down or otherwise register the

**To explore:**

- Promise and vow
- Oath and obligation
- Truth, trustworthiness, fidelity
- Initiation – before and after
- Old life – new life
- Secrets to conceal – secrets to contain
- Initiation to be experienced
- Binding and commitment

central part of what he is experiencing. The right word here is indeed experience, because there is very little of our ritual that cannot easily be read about in ritual books, which are freely on sale. And finally the aspirant acknowledges that, should he break this trust, he will forfeit the right to be a member of any society of men who prize honour and virtue above the externals of rank and fortune. The bond between the aspirant and Freemasonry is almost complete.

# 9 Poverty and Riches
## *Third degree audiences only*

*To have and have not*

'You will remember the peculiar moment you were received into Masonry, poor and penniless, and cheerfully embrace the opportunity of practising that virtue you have professed to admire.'

*Part of the address to the aspirant in the first degree at the north-east corner of the temple*

In the Christian Bible a very important question is put: 'For what is a man profited if he shall gain the whole world and lose his own soul?' This question also impacts on Freemasonry. We are warned that there are no free passages to be gained, that no appearance of outer material wealth is of so much value as inner riches, the richness of a spirit that senses the joy of uprightness and integrity of the Self. Freemasonry teaches us that this is a treasure beyond price.

And it starts early on in our initiation.

'Whom have you there?'

'Mr Smith, a poor candidate in a state of darkness, who now comes of his own free will and accord, properly prepared, humbly soliciting to be admitted to the mysteries and privileges of Freemasonry.'

The Brethren therefore have established that the aspirant is in a state of poverty, in darkness, is prepared, and comes in humility. Poverty, darkness, prepared, humble: these last three are in fact all aspects of the first – poverty.

Darkness. A state of deprivation. Of all our senses, the sense of sight is by far the most important in our daily existence. We can do much without the sense of hearing, or of taste, or of touch, because our eyes will guide us in many if not most of the areas where those senses would have informed us. The sun, the greatest source of light in our world, is also the bringer of life, life through light. On our planet, not much life can survive without the light and warmth of the sun. So light is by far the greatest of the natural phenomena sustaining us.

Prepared. When we speak of the aspirant being 'properly prepared' we clearly are not referring to the physical preparation undertaken by the Tyler outside the door of the temple. We are, however, referring first and foremost to the preparation that has been going on inside the aspirant, in his mind and in his heart, and this is a preparation that may have been going on for many years, for most of his life. If that preparation has been proceeding at the right level, the aspirant will have arrived at the point of understanding the worthlessness of material reward. 'Uninfluenced by mercenary or other unworthy motive' sets the seal on the importance of poverty as a virtue.

Humble. It is not our intention to humiliate a new aspirant by the apparently bizarre mode of his physical preparation. It is, however, our intention that he should come divested of pride, since pride will not further his moral advancement, nor will it make it easy for him to integrate into the brotherhood of which he wishes to be a part. As the first lecture tells us:

> We are morally instructed not to boast of anything, but to give heed to our ways, to walk uprightly and with humility before God, there being no station in life on which pride can with stability be founded.

But we have another intention: we put the aspirant in a *submissive* posture, by blindfolding, by disarranging his clothing, by the cable-tow, and by challenging him at various points on his journey. This is not to humiliate him; it is rather to remind him of his own need for humility.

To sum all of this up: poverty is to be seen as a virtue, of greater value than the apparent advantages enjoyed by a multi-millionaire. Being divested of worldly goods helps us on our quest for freedom and ensures that we seek sources other than material

**To explore:**

- Material wealth, riches of the spirit
- Advantages of darkness
- Disadvantage of material light
- Humility
- Outer preparation, inner preparation
- Virtue of submission
- Worldly status, inner strength
- Sight and insight

ones for nourishment. We are deprived of light, outwardly, so that we may seek inner light undistracted by the senses of the outer world. We are deprived of valuables, to remind us how unimportant they are. We are reminded that status, in society, in our jobs, or in any activity we may engage in, is of no importance. We are reminded to 'prize honour and virtue above the external advantages of rank and fortune'. We are reminded that humility will assist us, in a way that no other condition may even approach, to understand the basic truth of our own existence, and that moral progress, unimpeded by concerns about status or wealth, will be worthwhile to achieve. Once the blindfold has been removed, we may never forget that we can now see with more than our eyes, that light exists in different forms, that insight into situations or into other people around us, can be more telling by far in our onward progress, a progress towards moral truth and virtue.

# 10 Obedience, Responsibility and Wisdom
## *Second and third degree audiences only*

*To be your own man*

'Why wisdom, strength and beauty?'
'Wisdom to contrive, strength to support, and beauty to adorn.'
'Moralise them.'
'Wisdom to conduct us in all our undertakings, strength to support us under all our difficulties, and beauty to adorn the inward man.'

Someone said recently, 'Wisdom isn't valued much in today's world. Given a choice between being famous and being wise, many people would think there was no contest. Fame trumps wisdom, every time.' Is this true?

Let us examine the nature of wisdom. Wisdom is an understanding of the highest principle of things, that functions as a guide for living a truly exemplary life. In other words by wisdom we are enabled to live a life that avoids mistakes as far as possible, allowing us to make true moral progress towards our own perfection. When wisdom informs our reason, we become prudent in our actions. The ancient Greeks called prudence 'practical wisdom'. Nowadays, prudence in politics can mean doing whatever one can get away with, but a true application of prudence shows us something entirely apart: the difference between courage and rashness.

This may remind us of our situation at the door of the temple in the first degree when the poignard resisted our advance, and the cable-tow hindered our retreat. Prudence required then that we neither rushed forward nor held back. Steady, humble perseverance was the only course open to us. This lesson, when we submitted ourselves to those who directed our course, was the first lesson that Freemasonry taught us. It taught us how to 'conduct ourselves in all our undertakings' and thus instilled wisdom into our hearts.

But this was in a sense imposed obedience to authority. We were taught the virtue of humility, which underscores so much of conduct in Masonic matters. The authority to which we were then subject was the authority of the Master and the other officers in the lodge, exercising their duties to make sure that we passed correctly through the ceremony of our initiation. But it was also the authority of Masonic principles, to teach us to adhere to 'the Masonic line and rule', a new way of life that we had freely chosen, a way of life leading us away from selfish pursuits, passions and prejudices.

At the end of our initiation ceremony, we were instructed in other virtues 'to which your attention may be peculiarly and forcibly directed', and the three foremost were secrecy, fidelity and obedience. Up to then, in order to accept that authority and to exercise that obedience, a large measure of another characteristic had been required – trust. For us to exercise that trust we needed to place our confidence in our new-found Brethren, a confidence that they would act in our interests, a little like going into the operating theatre with a conviction that the surgeon is going to repair whatever is wrong.

In the first degree lodge, three *rule* a lodge. On embarking on the second degree, things are different. In a second degree lodge five *hold* a lodge, and the new Fellow Craft is one of the five, being now enabled to work with the square, level and plumb rule to encourage morality, equality, and justness and uprightness of life and actions. So now we are able to exercise our own *voluntary* obedience, in place of the *imposed* submission of the former degree.

But to earn the new-found responsibility for our own actions in the second degree, and to show that we merit it, something important has to happen: having started to free ourselves from passions and prejudices in the first degree, we now have to put right possible misdeeds from our past. We may have to atone for past wrongs, to make restitution for past misdemeanours. We go into the middle chamber ostensibly to receive our wages, but in order to do so, we must first pay our debts.

The entrance to the middle chamber is therefore a very important turning-point. As with initiation

> **To explore:**
>
> - The nature of wisdom
> - Importance of wise decisions
> - Importance of prudence
> - Imposed submission, voluntary obedience
> - Five holding a lodge
> - Paying debts
> - Earning credits
> - Turning points

itself, we will never be the same again. We pay our debts and receive the reward for doing so: our wages. These are of course wages of more than material worth. They are a spiritual reward for the moral progress we have so far made, progress away from our base, self-centred existence, progress away from the darkness of unknowing, towards light, towards the perfection of our Self. In the middle chamber we learn the name of God, and sense that we are drawing closer to Him.

We have begun to accept fully our responsibility for our actions. We have begun to be our own man.

# JOURNEYS

## 11 Pilgrimage

*Journey towards light*

After the prayer in the first degree, the aspirant is led round the temple by the Deacon in a clockwise manner, past the Master in the east, and halting at the Junior Warden and Senior Warden for an examination.

In times gone by, in all pursuits of self-discovery and self-improvement, as well as spiritual quests, a pilgrimage was necessary. In the ancient world, the deities who controlled certain areas of life were unable to operate outside those areas. Their power to favour or to destroy operated only within their own area. So a man from the mountains who found himself in the plain and was in need of divine help, had to make a pilgrimage back to his place of origin in order once again to be one with the deity controlling the mountainous regions. Pilgrimages therefore are journeys with a sacred or spiritual intent, and since the whole of Freemasonry is a journey, we have here a little pilgrimage, a part of that total journey.

This pilgrimage, however, is unique. It is that journey which, once the aspirant has moved away from the door of the temple, leads him away from worldly pursuits towards the abandonment of selfish goals, in order to draw nearer to his Self. It may also be regarded as a journey away from darkness towards light. It is a journey which he might undertake with apprehension, with a feeling that something unexpected might suddenly overtake him or confront him.

It is also a journey that he undertakes in personal darkness, since he is blindfolded. This blindfold is an allegory of two things: that his attention might be focused inwards rather than outwards, and also to underline his spiritual poverty. He has come here, he assures the

Master, to seek improvement, 'soliciting to be admitted to the mysteries and privileges of Freemasonry'. In ancient times of course a physical pilgrimage might have lasted many years and might have been accompanied by many dangers and difficulties, even life-threatening ones. The ritual of Freemasonry endeavours to represent this in an allegorical way.

In the eighteenth century in England, and even today in many Masonic jurisdictions, the Junior and Senior Wardens were placed, not as they are today in the south and the west respectively, but both of them in the west, either side of the entrance to the temple. In this situation, they acted as gate-keepers, guarding the entrance to the temple against unwanted intruders. They represented the Roman god Janus, the keeper of gates and doors, and hence representing also beginnings and endings, depicted by a double-faced head, one face looking out, the other face looking in. Janus was worshipped at the beginning of the harvest time, planting, marriage, birth, and other types of beginnings, especially the beginnings of important events in a person's life. Janus also represents the transition between primitive life and civilisation, and the growing to maturity of a young person.

We could try to imagine how these gate-keepers in an earlier century might have responded to an aspirant being brought to them by the Deacon. The question 'Whom have you there?' might have been delivered in a stern and forbidding tone, as if to say 'What do you want here? Why should I let you pass? Convince me that you are a worthy man, worthy enough to be admitted to our secrets and mysteries.'

Consider the Deacon's answer on

**To explore:**

• Journeying away
• Journeying towards
• What is a pilgrim/pilgrimage
• The point of journeying in darkness
• The nature and location of inward light
• A gate or door as a point of transition
• The help of God
• Freedom

behalf of the aspirant: 'Mr Smith, a poor aspirant in a state of darkness, who has been well and worthily recommended, regularly proposed and approved in open lodge, and now comes of his own free will and accord, properly prepared, humbly soliciting to be admitted to the mysteries and privileges of Freemasonry.' To condense this a little, what the Warden wants to hear is that the aspirant is well recommended, is approved of by all the members, comes of his own free will, that he is prepared not only outwardly but also inwardly and that he comes in humility. Humility is of course important, and is allied to the lack of rashness mentioned elsewhere in the ceremony.

But the gatekeeper's task is not yet done. By what means does this aspirant expect to gain such precious advancement? Or, in the words of the ritual, 'How does he hope to obtain those privileges?' The answer contains two essential features of admission to Freemasonry, namely that he seeks the help of God in his endeavour, and that he is free. Without these, initiation cannot proceed.

# 12 The Journeyman
## *Second and third degree audiences only*

*Pilgrimages to the centre*

'Did you ever travel?'
'My forefathers did.'
'Where did they travel?'
'Due east and west.'
'What was the object of their travels?'
'They travelled east in search of instruction, and west to propagate the knowledge they had gained.'

*Second section of the second lecture*

In some jurisdictions the Fellow Craft Freemason is called the Journeyman. The title derives from the medieval craftsman who, having worked his apprenticeship, was then obliged to travel in order to gain experience and to prove that he was qualified to do the work. In those present-day jurisdictions, the Journeyman is equipped with a sort of Masonic passport which he takes with him when visiting other lodges. The Secretary of the lodge so visited then stamps his passport to signify that he has made that journey. One of the qualifications for progressing to the next degree is the number of journeys the Journeyman has made in this way.

All of Freemasonry is a journey. Although for us it has a beginning at our initiation, it is a journey without end. We never arrive at the true destination, because the point of the journey is the travelling, the constant asking of questions, the constant unravelling and decoding of the symbols, during which we constantly grow in spirit. And one of the symbols is the pilgrimage itself, the perambulation round the temple which, though short and relatively uneventful, serves to remind us of how those in earlier times might have had to journey to find the true meaning of life and of the spirit.

On our entrance to the temple at the start of the second degree ceremony, we made our first pilgrimage directly after the prayer, without further announcement. This was a formalised way of demonstrating that we had been duly and truly initiated. We were examined by the Junior Warden. In the eighteenth century in England (and in many Masonic jurisdictions today) the Wardens were placed either side of the door of the temple in the west, the Junior at the south-west, the Senior at the north-west. Their function was that of gatekeepers, to control the entrance to the temple.

We might imagine them so situated and visualise the exchanges we have with them, the Junior Warden proving us first as a Freemason. At that level then, our pilgrimage was to affirm that we were qualified to enter, although only in our first degree status. But then we made a second pilgrimage, on the order of the Master, to prove that we were properly prepared for the onward journey through the second degree. Here, we proved ourselves to the Senior Warden that we were, to use a well-known phrase, in transit, in an in-between state, not yet qualified as a Fellow Craft, but journeying just the same, equipped with the key to open the door to the second degree lodge, namely the pass grip and password, whose import is represented by an ear of corn near to a fall of water, emblems of sustenance for our journey.

Now we made another, quite different journey, ascending a winding staircase. Not only did we ascend to a higher level by this journey, we completed one quarter of a circle, an angle of ninety degrees, changing direction according to the most important Masonic symbol, the square.

And this journey led us to the door of the middle chamber, that place where we go for three very important reasons. We progress to the middle chamber to purge old wrongs, in this way to repay any debts we may have, to repair wrongdoings and to make atonement. We progress to the middle chamber to enable us

> **To explore:**
>
> • The journey, the destination
> • The meaning and purpose of pilgrimage
> • Proving qualifications to ourselves and others
> • Ascent to another level
> • Turning points, literal and figurative
> • Nature of the middle chamber
> • Debits and credits
> • Approaching God

also to receive our wages, wages of a spiritual worth, rewards for the progress we have so far made in journeying away from the base impulses of our own lower nature, of overcoming passions and prejudices, and moving decisively away from darkness towards light.

But the third reason for our desire to progress to the middle chamber is that here, for the first time, we are approaching the Deity – here we become acquainted with the name of God, and here too we sense that our onward, upward journey is bringing us nearer to God Himself. The secrets of nature, our own nature, and the principles of intellectual truth, the truth within ourselves, are being unveiled to our view.

# 13 Journey to the Middle Chamber
## *Second and third degree audiences only*

*Turning the corner*

'After our ancient Brethren had entered the porch, they arrived at the foot of the winding staircase which led to the middle chamber. Their ascent was opposed by the Junior Warden, who demanded of them the password leading from the first to the second degree.'

*Part of the second degree tracing board lecture*

In other Masonic jurisdictions the Fellow Craft is called a Journeyman. This is because a craftsman in ancient times who had completed his apprenticeship then had to journey in order to find work, and to prove his skill as a craftsman to other Masters. His journeys therefore lasted several weeks, even months. Masonic allegorical journeys in the temple are much shorter, and this does not always give us the opportunity to experience the dimension that properly belongs to such journeys. We might try to expand them, in our mind, as we experience them, expand the single pilgrimage around the lodge, in our imagination, into an arduous journey of several weeks, working, and proving ourselves as we go.

We all know that Freemasonry is more particularly a series of journeys within journeys. Each of the three degrees is a journey, or pilgrimage, with lesser pilgrimages within it. But the second degree, in its entirety, represents the journey through life, that major part of our earthly existence between birth and death. It is that part of the composite Masonic journey which addresses increasing knowledge, wisdom, insight, and the payment of dues, both payment by us and to us.

Our figurative second degree journey starts by progressing round the temple, proving ourselves as Apprentices. This is necessary, because we need to remind ourselves, and prove to others, that we have begun the ascent out of our former life, a life based perhaps on nothing other than material concerns, towards a new moral and spiritual dimension.

Next, we progress again in order to prove, by the allegorical means of the password, that we have passed the transit stage and are able to be in harmony with this new, second degree lodge. By this second pilgrimage, we are acting out that transition stage represented by our ancient Brethren proving themselves to the Junior Warden inside the porch, at the foot of the winding staircase.

Our next journeying is heralded by the Master's words: 'Brother Senior Warden, you will direct the Senior Deacon to instruct the candidate to advance to the east in due form.' The aspirant will remember the way he approached the Master's pedestal in the first degree, and may well be expecting something similar. He could not, however, expect what is to follow. In the first degree, his advance was made on one level, and in a straight line, whereas here he ascends a winding staircase, passing through the fourth part of a circle, namely ninety degrees, the angle of the square.

We arrive at the Master's pedestal, emblematically the door of the middle chamber, where, in order to complete our journey, namely the journey into the middle chamber itself, we must first be in possession of the secrets of the second degree, those proofs that were demanded of our ancient Brethren before the Senior Warden would allow them to pass.

Let us sum all this up. We have completed our apprenticeship. We have confirmed our status as a qualified apprentice to ourselves and to the Brethren. The means of making the transition from a first degree lodge to one in the second degree have been given to us, and we have journeyed round the temple once again, proving that we are qualified to advance. Now that we are qualified we may advance to the east by passing up the winding staircase. At the top, we receive permission to enter the middle chamber.

And for what do we enter the middle chamber? To pay our debts in order to receive our spiritual wages. While there, we learn the name of God, and sense that, in a later onward advancement, we may achieve one-ness with Him. The journey is still a

**To explore:**

• Reasons for journeying
• Life as a journey
• Masonic pilgrimage, actual pilgrimage
• Ascending journeys
• Approaching the middle chamber
• Entering the middle chamber
• Debits and credits
• Allegory of the middle chamber

journey advancing, away from darkness towards light, but now it is also a journey ascending, as the angels on Jacob's ladder ascended to God, and teaches us, through the working tools of this degree, the means of making an advance in morality, stability, fidelity and uprightness.


# 14 Journey into the Unknown
### *Third degree audiences only*

*Through the darkness to greater light*

'The light of a Master Mason is darkness, visible, serving only to *express* that gloom which rests on the prospect of futurity. It is that

44

mysterious veil which the eye of human reason cannot penetrate, unless assisted by that light which is from above.'

*The charge after raising*

We undertake many journeys in Freemasonry. They are mostly different in quality, and different in intent, but they all lead us, eventually, away from darkness into light. Since they are allegorical journeys, not extended physical ones, they may lack the sense of a major pilgrimage lasting many days or years. We might try to imagine them as much longer, more arduous, in order to infuse them with a sense of something substantial achieved at the end.

Some journeys in Freemasonry seem to be complicated – we cannot always see the light towards which we are progressing. Of all our journeying, the journeys in the third degree are the most elaborate.

First, after leaving the temple entrusted with the password, we re-enter the intentionally darkened space, darkened not only for ourselves, but for all those present, and progress on the first pilgrimage round the temple to prove ourselves. We are thus proved as an Apprentice, reminding us of those duties we promised to undertake in the first degree, reminding us too of the need for moral progress, away from distractions of the world and towards the light of self-knowledge.

Then, in a similar pilgrimage, we progress round the temple to prove ourselves as a Fellow Craft, reminding us of further duties, but also reminding us of the fact that we had gained, through the time we had spent in the middle chamber, a measure of responsibility, a measure of maturity. It sought also to remind us that we had paid some debts there, in order to receive our wages, credits earned by the paying of debts, what we might call balancing the accounts.

The third pilgrimage was, symbolically, to prove that we had the necessary passport to make the transition from the second to the third degree, that our consciousness had been raised to the level necessary for us to be in harmony with this new level.

'Brother Senior Warden, you will direct the Deacons to instruct the candidate to advance to the east by the proper steps.' Thus the Master directed that we should undertake the next pilgrimage, the journey from the relative security of second degree status, plunging us into something unknown and, in many respects, completely unexpected. We had to negotiate an obstacle, an obstacle associated with the figurative death of our Self. And although the physical distance covered in this pilgrimage was shorter than in the others, yet symbolically we travelled much farther, across the very symbol of death. We travelled, figuratively, as far as Hercules travelled, into the underworld to vanquish the power of evil.

Had we not earlier been promised light and enlightenment on our Masonic journey, we might at this point have felt very apprehensive. A pilgrimage apparently leading to the underworld is not to be undertaken lightly. 'It is but fair to inform you that a most serious trial of your fortitude and fidelity, and a more solemn obligation await you.' These words indicate that we must sink still lower, arriving at a true appreciation of the death of the Self, before we can be reborn at a higher level of awareness, of morality, and of self-knowledge. Our journey therefore is still a downward one, reaching, at its end, into the grave itself, where we may bury our old, material Self.

But, as we now know, the last figurative journey in this degree leads us upward again, towards the greatest light of self-knowledge. In the sanctum sanctorum, where our base Self is *not* buried, we come face to face with God. Aided by divine light

**To explore:**

- Reasons for journeying
- Need to prove ourselves in earlier degrees
- Aspects of the journey over the grave
- Overcoming obstacles
- The 'death' of the Self
- Journeying upwards from death
- One-ness with God
- The vital and immortal principle

and wisdom we have pierced the veil. We have lifted our eyes to God's hope for us, the bright morning star. We have trampled evil underfoot. We are now listening to the voice of our own purified nature and are coming to know our own vital and immortal principle, that light and goodness of which we are personally capable.

## 15 From the Mystique to the Mystical
### *Third degree audiences only*

*Setting aside the novelty*

'Proceeding onwards, still guiding your progress by the principles of *moral* truth, you were led, in the second degree, to contemplate the *intellectual* faculty, and to trace it, from its development, through the paths of heavenly science, even to the throne of God Himself. The secrets of nature, and the principles of intellectual truth were then unveiled to your view.'

*Exhortation in the third degree*

There are many occasions and many situations in which non-Masons have sought to ridicule Freemasonry for practices which they, erroneously, have perceived as bizarre or laughable. Among these are the idea that adults, and particularly men, wear aprons; that they bare one knee; that the initiation ceremony involves the use of a blindfold, that Freemasons have an incongruous handshake and bizarre signs; that they gain unfair advantages in society and in their careers.

It is easy to dismiss all this as uninformed chatter, even perhaps envy, but it is not unknown for initiates themselves to feel slightly embarrassed about the arcane aspects of initiation. Happily, many more aspirants for all the degrees have felt the excitement of the unknown, of the mystique of what they were experiencing. But is that acquaintance with, and eagerness to know, the mystique really enough? The answer is that mystique, if not properly channelled and explained, can remain unfruitful, and rewarding only at a superficial level. Let us tease out some of this mystique and put it under our microscope.

We were blindfolded and led to a door, where unfamiliar knocks gained admission. We had to declare that we were 'free' before being led round and challenged as to our qualification to proceed. After taking some seemingly incongruous steps forward, we made a vow of fidelity, and were instructed in regard to 'secrets'. We were instructed in allegories of the sun, moon and stars. We ascended a winding staircase into a 'middle chamber'. We stepped over an open grave, and were afterwards lowered into it. And finally, we were raised up again and taught about our arrival in the sanctum sanctorum. Each of these landmarks, and others, had a vital lesson to impart, without which the Masonic journey would not have been completely fulfilling.

The blindfold did not *conceal* something we were supposed *not* to see. By removing outer distractions, it sought to give us another perspective, another point of view, namely the focus for the search of self-knowledge, the point within ourselves, the centre of the circle, to discover, in the words of the ritual, that 'point from which we cannot err'.

In this state, we passed a threshold, namely the boundary between that material world outside the temple, and that inner sanctum of holiness and peace within, where no distractions were present to divert us from our course of seeking inner light. We strove for freedom from selfish concerns and unworthy thoughts and passions, and freedom from the desire of things of material worth, so as to know the desire for moral progress and fulfilment. We stated that we were free, in the words of the lecture 'free *to* good fellowship, and ought to be free *from* vice', but this was not necessarily the state we were *in*, rather the state to which we *aspired*.

We were challenged as to our fitness to proceed on this quest for perfection, since without a challenge, we could not prove to ourselves how serious we were in our endeavour. We made a vow of fidelity, since without committing ourselves to the purpose of our journey, and without binding ourselves to the fraternity with others, we were like a rudderless ship, with no course to steer, and no means of steering either. The secrets to which we bound ourselves in this way were not mere handshakes, signs and words; they were the secrets we gained through our experience, the insights governing our hearts, insights leading to moral growth and development.

The rising sun was for us an emblem of birth, growth and inner light, enlightenment of the heart; the moon, an emblem of the onset of night and of inevitable death; the stars, an emblem of the promise of immortality and the one-ness of the celestial and terrestrial realms. We were able to approach heaven by ascending the winding staircase, and to enter the middle chamber to pay debts and receive wages.

But while engaged in this ascent to heavenly realms, we were suddenly reminded of our own physical mortality, and attempted to tread our old, unregenerated self underfoot by stepping over the grave. We were reminded that our newly regenerated self could achieve

> **To explore:**
>
> • Differences between mystique and mystical
> • The purpose and effect of the blindfold
> • Outside the temple – inside the temple
> • Commitment and binding
> • Freedom and commitment
> • Real secrets
> • Heaven and earth
> • Crossing the grave, rising from it

immortality, by again being raised from that same grave, and by being allowed to pierce the mysterious veil shielding us from that immortality, so that we might lift our eyes to that bright horizon that might await us if we persevered in our search for spiritual growth and perfection.

It was then, once we had arrived in the sanctum sanctorum, that we could come face to face with God, and could own our one-ness with Him. It was then only that we had left behind the mystique, and had come to understand the mystical.

# SYMBOLS AND TOOLS

## 16 Ornaments, Furniture and Jewels

*Decorating the edifice*

The ornaments of a Freemason's Lodge are the mosaic pavement, the blazing star and the indented or tessellated border; the furniture is the Volume of the Sacred Law, the Compasses and Square; the movable jewels are the square, level and plumb rule; the immovable jewels are the tracing board, the rough ashlar and the perfect ashlar.

Freemasonry is about allegory, allusion, parable, oblique hints, intimations. The fun and the fascination for Freemasons is in teasing out the meanings, in decoding the symbols. That is to say, it starts out as fun and fascination, but quickly we learn that the resulting answers, the fruits of our work in decrypting the many-sided marks, signs and tokens, prove to be enriching for us in our lives, our very existence.

From a geometrical point of view, the triangle is the most stable of two-dimensional forms and, unlike the square and many other forms, cannot be distorted – as long as the three sides remain firm and straight, the angles are constant. And many times in Freemasonry we meet with the number three, and many times the objects we study exist in groups of three, triangles in which each part is dependent on the other two.

'Of what is the interior of a Freemason's lodge composed?' asks the question in the first lecture. 'Ornaments, furniture and jewels' is the answer. The first part of this triad, the ornaments of the lodge, are the mosaic pavement, the blazing star and the tessellated border. The mosaic pavement, the black and white squares, represent the opposites in life, the two ends of the spectrum, black and white intimating evil and good, tragedy and good fortune, death and life.

But unlike the two ends of the spectrum, which are separated by the intervening colours, here the black and the white sit side by side, a reminder of how close success is to failure, how good fortune and bad are often companions.

The blazing star is related to the mosaic pavement, and represents divine light, the One. This all-powerful force tells us that of the black and white squares, the white – the light – can overcome darkness, evil and death, and so it stands on its own, unadorned, the purest intimation of good. The tessellated border binds everything in the lodge, being situated at the outer limits, and emblematically binds also the objects on the tracing board.

The second part of the triad is the furniture of the lodge: the Volume of the Sacred Law, the compasses and square. These are elsewhere called the three great lights, but note the order in which they appear here – the compasses before the square, not after. This represents their relative importance, in descending order. The sacred volume is representative of God's revealed will to man, and is the surest proof of God's beneficence to us. The compasses circumscribe the circle, the centre being the point from which we cannot err, so one leg is placed on that centre, a point designated by God, the point from which we originate; the other leg describes the circumference, the bounds of moral conduct, encompassing that area in which we have our dealings with our fellow-men.

The movable jewels are the square, level and plumb rule. After the triangle, the square is one of the most interesting forms. Our instinct tells us that of all geometrical forms, the right angle is the one which best represents correctness, regularity, integrity. As the lecture tells us: 'The square teaches us to regulate our lives and actions according to the Masonic line and rule,' (universal morality) 'and to harmonise our conduct in this life.'

So too the level instils in us the virtue of regarding each other as equals, not to be tempted to regard others as in any way inferior to us and, importantly, not to regard ourselves as being in any way not up to the mark. Self-esteem, not pride, is important in this. The plumb rule completes the triad. The lecture refers to it as 'the *infallible plumb rule*' which, like Jacob's ladder, connects heaven and earth, and is the criterion of truth. It is described as infallible because, being governed by the force of gravity, it will always indicate the same point, the centre of the earth.

The immovable jewels of the lodge lie open in the lodge for us to moralise on. These are the tracing board and the rough and perfect ashlars. If we consider these from the point of view of the operative Mason, the tracing board is that place where the design

> **To explore:**
>
> • The purpose of allegory
> • The triangle and the square
> • The purpose of adornment
> • Black and white opposing
> • Binding together
> • The two legs of the compasses
> • The plumb rule
> • From rough ashlar to perfect ashlar

is created, the rough ashlar is that object representing our first attempts at forming a stone to be incorporated in the building, and the perfect ashlar the completed stone ready to be placed. So too in an allegorical sense, the tracing board, like the Volume of the Sacred Law, is where the design for our lives and actions originates; the rough ashlar represents our first attempts at forming ourselves, and the perfect ashlar may represent what we hope, eventually, to achieve.

# 17 Naming Tools

*Preparing the work*

'The working tools of an Entered Apprentice Freemason are the twenty-four inch gauge, the common gavel and chisel. The twenty-four inch gauge is to measure our work; the common gavel to knock off all superfluous excrescences, and the chisel to further smooth and prepare the stone, and render it fit for the hands of the more expert workman.'

*Part of the presentation of the working tools in the first degree*

In the presentation of the working tools, the Master first describes their use as operative, concrete tools, physical attributes displayed, so that we can first impress on our minds how the world sees such tools. Once he has finished, he tells us: 'But as we are not all operative Masons, but rather free and accepted, or speculative, we apply these tools to our morals', and he then proceeds to an exposition of them as speculative tools. The definition of the word 'speculate' appropriate to Masonic symbolism is 'to observe or view mentally; to consider or reflect upon with close attention; to contemplate' and the word itself comes from Latin *speculari* meaning to spy out, or watch.

This is particularly appropriate to allegories, since an allegory is a description of some subject under the guise of another of suggestive similarity. A cupid shoots an arrow into a heart, and someone is said to be love struck! In Freemasonry, we can look at a plumb rule and, seeing a tool which tests whether an object is upright, can see in it a symbol which we can memorise and then use to remind ourselves when our actions are perhaps not as virtuous or as principled as they might be. And so we have the three working tools in the first degree, but note that these are not tools of construction; they are tools of preparation, to prepare the rough ashlar, and 'render it fit for the hands of the more expert workman'.

When we contemplate, these three tools form a remarkable triad. The gavel may be said to represent man's driving, passionate nature. We often speak of a person as 'a man of action', meaning that he is not content to sit still and let things happen – a laudable characteristic in itself. He is constantly striving; striving either to further his own aims, or striving to combat negative forces, threats and dangers. But such a person may not contemplate the consequences of all his activity. He may appear to us to be lacking in judgement or wisdom. He may also be the kind of person who gives full rein to impulses, passions and prejudices.

The chisel is a very interesting tool. It seems to be entirely inert, passively enduring the strokes of the gavel, bearing all the blows rained down on it. Yet this tool is capable of very fine work. It not only receives the blows, but transmits them to the stone, transforming them into detailed and beautiful working of the design to be carved. It is able to determine the course of the line being carved, and therefore represents man's creative, analytical nature, a tool which seeks to give expression to a person's finer feelings. Although it is driven by the gavel, it alone is responsible for the way the finer part of the work proceeds.

It is not at first apparent how the twenty-four inch gauge relates to the other two, until we consider what happens when the gavel delivers too much force, and then the line cut will go too far, or too deep, or too much stone will be removed. The twenty-four inch gauge is there, in this instance, to tell the workman to curb the gavel, as it is also there to inform the workman if the chisel does not cut far enough or deep enough. The resulting work must fit into the measures required of it by the gauge.

So the twenty-four inch gauge is present to act to *restrain* the gavel, to prompt it to deliver *measured* blows, but also to *encourage* the chisel, to assist it to overcome some natural diffidence and to assert its own creativity a little more. And so it is in our speculation, our contemplation – once our passionate, driving nature has been reminded to stop at the right place, to stop short of excess, and once our sensitive, analytical, creative impulses have been encouraged to greater assertiveness, then we shall lead a *measured* existence, measured in more than one sense.

**To explore:**

• Speculation
• From speculative to operational
• What allegories are for
• Tools to prepare, not to build
• Impulses and passions
• Action and contemplation
• The chisel in analysing and creating
• Different aspects of measuring

# 18 Tracing the Grand Design

*Laying out the symbols*

The tracing boards are the visual means by which our attention is drawn to Masonic symbolism. The many symbols depicted on them are interlinked, and provide a visual image that we can translate into a figurative insight for our lives.

From earliest Masonic systems we see the practice of tracing on the floor of the lodge the symbols of each degree, and the custom of Masters to illustrate the subject of their lecture by reference to drawings. The earliest practice was for the Master to demonstrate the symbolism and allegory by drawing designs on the floor of the lodge with chalk, which the Tyler would erase when the lodge was closed. Nowadays, the form of the tracing boards has become standardised as rigid boards painted with the symbols and allegories of each degree. To enable the board to be of use to all the members of the lodge, it is laid flat on the floor in the middle of the temple.

For symbolism to be most effective, let us start with the most important and trace the allegories through the degree. The central symbols on the first degree board are not the most prominent ones depicted; they are the three great lights in Freemasonry, the Volume of the Sacred Law, the square and compasses, which are found on the pedestal depicted near the bottom of the board.

> 'The sacred writings are to govern our faith, the square to regulate our actions, and the compasses to keep us in due bounds with all mankind, particularly our Brethren in Freemasonry.'

The first then concerns God's dealings with humankind; the second, the square, is an emblem of correct morality, the most central and most important symbol in Freemasonry.

Morality informs us as to the distinction between right and wrong, between good and evil, in relation to our actions, our intentions or our character. The square is 'to regulate our actions' and this happens on many different levels. It teaches us to harmonise our conduct, a way of making the right music. The right angle is in one sense the most true angle – any other, less than or more than ninety degrees, is an angle that is indeterminate. A right angle is one we know by instinct to be true, and truth is at the heart of much insight in Freemasonry.

Near the bottom right-hand corner of the tracing board lie the square, level and plumb rule. The square is also that emblem formed by setting the plumb rule, the symbol of uprightness, next to the level, the symbol of equality, the upright and the level together forming an angle of ninety degrees. So morality can be seen as the product of level dealings allied to upright conduct. The square is repeatedly brought to our attention as an emblem of morality. The Master tells us in the first degree:

> 'You are therefore expected to stand perfectly erect, your feet formed in a square, your body being thus considered

an emblem of your mind and your feet of the rectitude of your actions.'

We then form two right angles – one with our feet, and the other being the angle formed between our upright frame and the level ground. When we speak of being 'demoralised' we may mean more than just 'downhearted'. We may mean that we are having difficulty maintaining an upright position; that we can no longer maintain the angle of ninety degrees which our uprightness would call for, and that our morale, if not our morality, is not in a good position.

Of other images of uprightness on the tracing board, the three most prominent are the three great pillars supporting a Freemason's lodge: those of wisdom, strength and beauty. Note that these also form a right angle with the ground on which they stand, namely the chequered pavement.

> **To explore:**
>
> • Must all allegories be visual?
> • Relationship of the three great lights to each other
> • Further examples of the square in the lodge
> • The nature of morality
> • Harmony, regular conduct
> • True angles; true morality; truth
> • Relation of the square to the level and the plumb rule
> • Wisdom, strength and beauty in life

In terms of morality then, these three have three important lessons for us. The Ionic column, the furthest away on the tracing board, represents wisdom, and the figure surmounting it is that of King Solomon, who established Jerusalem as the city of justice and peace. He was said to have been given both wisdom and knowledge by God, and he embodies the ability to distinguish between good and evil. The pillar nearest to us on the tracing board is the Doric, representing strength, surmounted by the figure of Hiram, King of Tyre. The middle pillar is the Corinthian column, said to represent Hiram Abiff, the principal architect of King Solomon's temple, representing therefore beauty, 'to adorn the inward man'. These pillars are said to support a Freemason's lodge. In our building, we construct two edifices – one is the temple to humanity which we seek to construct in concert with our Brethren; the other is our own moral edifice, and in either sense, we should remember that wisdom, strength and beauty are our chief supports.

# 19 Ornaments of the Lodge
*Third degree audiences only*

*Aids to construction*

The interior of a Freemason's lodge is composed of ornaments, furniture and jewels. These are catalysts for our building, not directly involved, but essential nonetheless.

Ornaments are there to adorn the lodge, but have also their own symbolic significance. In the Entered Apprentice's lodge the ornaments are the mosaic pavement, the blazing star and the tessellated border. Man is born out of darkness, and physically he returns to darkness at death. Life, the God-given consciousness that makes us what we are, is full of light, represented by the white squares, light of varying kinds, of varying intensities.

We speak of the mosaic pavement, the beautiful flooring of the lodge. The technique of making mosaic pavements is to compose a design for a floor or wall decoration out of many different colours, sizes, shapes and materials to form a design or picture. This seems at variance with our rather sober chequerboard design of alternating white and black squares, where only two colours and one shape and size are employed, but herein lies its intensity. There is no opportunity for our artistic licence or fantasy to take flight. Freemasonry has reduced its mosaic composition to a very sparse, bare design, but it is this very sparseness, this spartan quality, that makes it so arresting. Light and darkness. White and black. Good and evil. Joy and sorrow. Well-being and sickness. Riches and poverty. Life and death. Light and darkness.

We all know that there are other colours, other shapes in the design of life. But here we wish to see how important it is that light triumphs over darkness, and to remind ourselves, first and foremost, of the power granted to us by the restoration of light at our initiation. We may well consider then that the pursuit of light in our lives, for ourselves and for our fellowmen, is of the first importance, and that spiritual progress, development, is made possible through a constant increasing of light in our lives and actions.

The blazing star, elsewhere called the glory, the second of the first degree ornaments, is also that which is referred to in the second degree closing:

'In this position, what have you discovered?'

'A sacred symbol.'

'Where is it situated?'

'In the centre of the building.'

And so this refers to God, the divinity at our own centre, the divinity which we seek on our Masonic path. The tessellated border, the third ornament, is to be found as the frame of the first degree tracing board, and therefore binds together the symbols of the first degree, ensuring that, like the secrets of Freemasonry, they are contained so as not to be dissipated.

The ornaments of a Master Mason's lodge are referred to in the ritual as the porch, dormer and square pavement. The porch represents one of the three thresholds in Freemasonry. In the first degree, the threshold was the door of the temple, that place of great import and danger for us, a threshold which had to be crossed so as to leave behind our base Self and start on our return to God and holiness. In the second degree the threshold was the door giving access to the middle chamber, access to knowledge and the intellect of the heart, knowing or gnosis. Here in the third degree is another doorway, that giving onto the sanctum sanctorum, the holy of holies, that place where we may stand face to face with God and understand our own worth, and our own destiny.

The dormer is the window that gives light to the sanctum sanctorum, through which streams God's healing and revealing light to make us whole

**To explore:**

• Elements of the design of life
• Black and white
• How light banishes darkness
• The power of light
• Light at the centre
• A border binds the whole
• Three thresholds
• Mosaic pavement in the first and third degrees

after we have been through the trials of the figurative death of the third degree. It again represents the light of birth, this time a rebirth, a light so powerful that it cannot be denied.

In the first degree, we were shown Jacob's ladder, but we did not ascend it. It was a promise of how we might ascend from earth to heaven, or from our own base Self to a purified, higher sense of being. In the second degree, we started our ascent by climbing the winding staircase, leaving the mosaic pavement behind. On that new level, the level of the middle chamber, there was no square pavement evident, and so we might be forgiven for thinking that we had left it behind. The third degree, however, makes all clear – on entering the sanctum sanctorum, on the same level as the middle chamber, we rediscover the square pavement, in exactly the same form as that of the Entered Apprentice's degree. Here, in our new, heightened state of consciousness, on our emergence from the tomb to a new life, we might come to regard in a new light the contrast of black and white, death and life.

# 20 Tools to Take Us Forward
## *Third degree audiences only*

*Implements advancing the work*

'But as we are not all operative Masons but rather free and accepted or speculative, we apply these tools to our morals.'

*Part of the presentation of the working tools in all degrees*

The tools which operative stonemasons use are of different categories. Some are tools for preparing the work, such as gavels, chisels, gouges, saws, augers. Some are tools used in actual construction, such as trowels, hawks, cramps, setting mauls. Some are tools used in checking the work, such as straight edges, squares, levels, bevels, plumb rules, compasses. And yet others are tools of creativity, such as pencils, compasses again, lettering chisels and others.

Within the three degrees of Freemasonry we have most of the tools mentioned and we can see their relation to actual, operative stonemasonry. Where we may need some guidance is in identifying their moral tendency, in contemplating on their real import for us on our Masonic journey.

The first thing to notice is that the tools we employ in the first degree are tools of preparation. Remember the words of the Master in the third degree in his retrospective of the first:

'It inculcated the useful lessons of natural equality and mutual dependence; it instructed you in the active principles of universal beneficence and charity . . . above all, it taught you to bend with humility and resignation to the will of the Great Architect of the Universe...'

Our hearts are thereby fitted, by the first degree, for the reception of truth and wisdom. The first degree, therefore, may be regarded as the stage before the building proper is embarked on. It may be regarded as the phase of preparation, and so the tools of this degree are tools which will assist in that preparation.

The gavel, representing our impelling, motivating instincts, impacts on the chisel, representing our sensitive, creative instincts. The twenty-four inch gauge represents the need to co-ordinate those two forces, to restrain, if need be, the driving, forceful side of our nature, and to stimulate, if need be, our passive, sensitive, creative nature.

Now let us consider the second degree, and let us once again listen to the words of the Master's retrospective:

'Proceeding onwards, still guiding your progress by the principles of *moral* truth, you were led, in the second degree, to contemplate the *intellectual* faculty, and to trace it, from its development, through the paths of heavenly science...'

These words need a little interpretation. Intellect refers not to academic excellence, but to the intellect of the heart, the virtue of instinct, feeling, intuition. The secrets of nature are the secrets of our own nature, so that intellectual truth refers to the truth we come to acknowledge in our own heart.

The tools we are going to need in this second degree pursuit will be tools to test the rightness of what we have learned. Since the square verifies the accuracy of square corners, the level the accuracy of horizontal parts of the structure and the plumb rule the accuracy of the vertical parts, so in like manner we need to verify that our moral progress is proceeding well, that we are dealing with our fellow men in a calm, steady, even-tempered way, and that our actions and intentions are upright ones. Uprightness, represented by the plumb rule, is another allegory, like Jacob's ladder and the hexalpha, that the two worlds, celestial and terrestrial, are linked, and that we may pass between them in our quest for greater moral and spiritual progress.

Arrived at the third degree, we have built much of the edifice of moral truth and virtue. We have tested its correctness with the knowledge we have gained, the secrets of nature and knowledge of ourselves. Now that we have passed through the third degree, now that we have trodden evil underfoot and lifted our eyes to the bright morning star, now is the time to decorate and adorn the building, to beautify what we have achieved. The skirret enables us to delineate the extent of the design; with the pencil we can design the decoration; with the compasses we can determine limits and proportions, to enable us to live a life of harmony, recognising the limits of good and evil.

**To explore:**

- Different uses of different tools
- Operative tools, speculative tools
- Speculative function of first-degree tools
- Moral truth leading to knowledge of the self
- Speculative function of second-degree tools
- Knowledge of the self-leading to the throne of God
- Speculative function of third-degree tools
- The need to beautify and adorn

# DARKNESS AND LIGHT

## 21 A State of Darkness

*Poverty and humility*

'Whom have you there?'

'Mr Smith, a poor candidate in a state of darkness… who now comes of his own free will, humbly soliciting to be admitted…'

*Exchange at the door of the temple in the first degree*

Elsewhere we speak of journeying from darkness to light. That allegory is an echo of another – the allegory of the aspirant's physical state of darkness. This may represent the darkness of un-knowing, the state in which the aspirant first entered the world. This darkness may also represent the state he is in before spiritual birth.

Darkness can indeed be a positive quality. First of all, as we know, darkness here ensures that there will be no outside distractions, so that the aspirant can focus inwardly, look at himself, start to have an appreciation of his own person, with his merits, certainly, but also his faults, his failings.

Then, of course, darkness also hides. Sometimes it can hide unpalatable truths from the aspirant, aspects of himself and his life that he prefers not to think about. Finding these, and facing them, will be a step on the path to truth, the third of the three Grand Principles on which Freemasonry is founded. But darkness can also hide other, more welcome influences. Up to now, the aspirant may not have been aware of the benefits to himself of exploring his own spiritual dimension – now he has the chance. By darkness he may be enabled to discover the blessings of inner silence and stillness. Because he cannot see, he will form no preconceived notions – he will be able to accept what happens to him with a good grace.

But most importantly, darkness is that which comes before the dawn. Darkness is that state, the state before birth, when we are unencumbered by ideas that are untrue. Darkness, confusion, comes before enlightenment. Let us examine this. We all know what it is like suddenly to experience something which makes sense out of seeming non-sense. We look perhaps for a way out of a problem or dilemma, and suddenly find the solution staring us in the face. So it is for our aspirant. What he aspires to here, in his journey from darkness to light, is perhaps not so sudden, but a gradual unfolding of self-awareness, self-knowledge and moral progress, so that he may, at least inwardly, be saying 'I never knew it could mean this.' What he may wish for is light, the light of knowledge.

The aspirant is called poor. Poverty is of two kinds – positive and negative. Material poverty should ensure that he is unencumbered by thoughts of how to make his life ever more full of luxuries and trivia. The fact that he has been deprived of money and valuables should mean that he will learn to appreciate the richness of his own spirit, unhindered by the acquisition of wealth and the material power that sometimes goes with it.

But when the Tyler announces that the aspirant is poor, he refers also to the fact that he has acknowledged his spiritual poverty, that the reason he comes to the lodge is to seek to advance his own spirit, to come to know himself, and through that to make for himself some moral advancement. The knowledge he lacks is knowledge of himself. The advancement he seeks is that which will become possible through self-knowledge.

The aspirant may never have regarded himself as poor in this regard. Indeed, he may never have considered his own spiritual dimension at all. Later on, we physically restore him to light, not gradually, but in a sharp realisation of the power of light, to show him allegorically what may await him during his Masonic journeying.

'...of his own free will, humbly soliciting to be admitted to the mysteries and privileges of Freemasonry'. He journeys freely, and in another essay we speak of the vital importance of freedom. But he also journeys humbly, and humility is an important quality. It is not to be confused with humiliation. Humility is not the giving up of riches, or of personal gifts. It is not the relinquishing of the aspirant's rights. It is an attitude of mind in which he figuratively lays himself bare; he lays claim to nothing more than his essential qualities. It is the quality of being at peace with very little. He wishes for light, but recognises his spiritual darkness, and is unencumbered by grand ideas, particularly ideas about material riches. Humility is the acknowledgement that pride will only hinder his progress towards knowledge. As the lecture puts it 'there is no station in life on which pride can with stability be founded'. He should progress with perseverance, but not rashly. Humility is an essential qualification.

> **To explore:**
>
> • Your own ideas of progress towards light
> • Darkness – a curse or a blessing?
> • Poverty – good and bad
> • Your own ideas of being deprived materially; positive and negative aspects
> • Your own ideas of being deprived spiritually
> • Un-knowing to knowing
> • Humility – laying claim to nothing
> • Humility – constraining or liberating?

# 22 Approaching Light

Steps forward

'Brother Senior Warden, you will direct the Junior Deacon to instruct the candidate to advance to the pedestal in due form.'

*After the first pilgrimage in the first degree*

Advance. The aspirant has already completed his first course of pilgrimage and now he is at his original starting point in the west, facing east. Accompanied still by the Junior Deacon he now progresses up the north side of the temple towards the east. Once he is in front of the Master, the Junior Deacon instructs him to place his feet at a right angle, 'in the form of a square'. The right angle, being a symbol of rectitude, is a very important symbol indeed. This is the first of many occasions on which the aspirant will be made acquainted with the square, both as a geometrical figure and as a working implement, and his repeated encounters with it will imprint on his mind and heart its paramount importance in leading him to a true appreciation of rectitude and regularity in life and actions.

Assisted by the Deacon, the aspirant now completes three steps forward towards the Master, the pedestal, and therefore the three great lights reposing on the pedestal. These steps may be regarded as an echo, a reminder of the balance we speak about in another essay, a balance between impetuosity and reticence. The first step, a small one, taken falteringly because the aspirant cannot see, may perhaps end with the aspirant's feet not being completely in the right position – the Deacon will correct this. By now the aspirant is probably able to get the measure of what is expected of him, and so the next step, not so reticent, a little longer than the first, will probably be accomplished with more confidence. His feet now form the second square. 'Another,' says the Deacon, 'still longer, heels together as before.' So now this third step is accomplished with yet more confidence, but, importantly, a confidence still tempered with humility, and lacking any trace of impetuosity. These steps therefore are 'measured' in both senses of the word.

Of course, the aspirant does not know that he is approaching light, but the Brethren in the temple do know this. They know that he is approaching not only the physical light at the Master's pedestal, but also the symbolic light of the three great lights, namely the Volume of the Sacred Law, the square and compasses. Here it is important that the Brethren know and recognise that this is happening, since by doing so, they are taking part in, assisting at, the aspirant's advance in spirituality.

> 'It is my duty to inform you that Masonry is free, and requires a perfect freedom of inclination in every candidate for its mysteries. It is founded on the purest principles of piety and virtue. It possesses great and invaluable privileges, and to secure those privileges to worthy men, vows of fidelity are required; but let me assure you that in those vows there is nothing incompatible with your civil, moral or religious duties.'

*Exhortation of the Master before the vow is made*

Once again, the aspect of freedom comes to the fore, but this time followed by piety and by virtue. By piety we mean obedience to the Deity, and reverence towards God in our attitude. Elsewhere the

| **To explore:** |
| --- |
| • What a square might mean as a symbol or allegory |
| • Increasing confidence on a journey |
| • The part played by the lodge members in the aspirant's progress |
| • Piety and virtue |
| • Privilege – outward, inward |
| • Building a person |
| • Meaning of 'worthy' |
| • Advantages gained by Freemasonry |

lecture exhorts us 'to love and adore God with an unrivalled and disinterested affection...' When this is combined with virtue, we have a powerful way of linking the aspirant into a supremely good moral system, since virtue consists in an observance of the recognised moral laws or standards of right conduct.

Freemasonry clearly does not confer any social or statutory privileges – no man advances in the profane world by virtue of being a Freemason. Nevertheless, as a Freemason, the aspirant will be privileged, and the greatest privilege for him will be that of being able to work with his Brethren in building his own moral and spiritual edifice and, with that, of contributing to the moral and spiritual edifice of humanity as a whole. So the privileges referred to here are the benefits and powers which the aspirant obtains by joining an organisation which shows him the way to enlightenment. It is quite a privilege for the aspirant to be accepted as an acolyte by his fellow Freemasons.

And so the Master declares that these privileges, constituting a route to enlightenment and moral progress, are to be accorded only to worthy men. The aspirant has proved himself worthy by his affirmative replies to the questions up to now in his initiation.

# 23 Light and Lights

*Three to guide*

'Having been kept for a considerable time in a state of darkness, what, in your present situation, is the predominant wish of your heart?'

'Light.'

'Brother Junior Deacon, let that blessing be restored to the candidate.'

*After the aspirant has made his vow in the first degree*

Many people regard this moment as the most crucial, the most poignant moment in the initiation ceremony, if not in the whole Masonic experience. The aspirant answers 'Light', and in this seems to be encapsulated his longing for the light of knowledge, of truth in himself. But before we study the answer, let us look again at the question.

In fact, it is necessary to read the question on two different levels. 'Having been kept for a considerable time in a state of darkness, what, in your present situation, is the predominant wish of your heart?' Does the Master refer only to the period that the aspirant has been blindfolded? Certainly he does mean that, but here we may consider a further, greater meaning. If we regard the aspirant's journey thus far as being a journey away from darkness, the darkness of the unenlightened state, a state where his own selfish impulses may have guided him, where he may not be free to set those aside and serve his fellow men selflessly, then he may well agree that he has been 'for a considerable time in a state of darkness', namely for much of his life up to now.

Consider for a moment the course of the aspirant's progress so far. He has entered the temple in the west, the place of the setting sun, and therefore the place of darkness. He has been led round the temple once, proving himself to the Wardens as he progressed, but he did not stay in the east – he returned to the west, because he was not yet ready to approach the light. Because he is blindfolded, he does not know that in the east, the place of the rising sun and therefore of life, the three great lights are placed, those symbols whose allegory will be of most importance to him on his journey.

Now he has been instructed how to approach the east, by the three level steps. He has already been told, in the prayer, that he may 'unfold the beauties of true godliness', and may have begun to perceive that as an increase of light, or enlightenment. He has been told by the Master that Freemasonry possesses 'great and invaluable privileges', and he may have a sense already that those privileges may encompass such enlightenment. He has made his vow. In it, he binds himself not to do anything whereby the secrets may become known to others by revealing them *to the light*, whereby they may be seen by others, since their true value may lie in being able to see them with the heart, rather than with the eyes.

So the aspirant is restored to material light, and at this point, before his attention is distracted by outward influences, the Master directs him to the three great lights in Freemasonry, the Volume of the Sacred Law, the square and compasses.

The Sacred Volume is the greatest of the three great lights. It represents the revealed will of God. It is spoken of as the greatest, since in all of Freemasonry, our ultimate goal is to focus on our relationship with God. The aspirant may here once more remember the prayer: '...that he may the better be enabled to unfold the beauties of true godliness...' and in the other degrees this union with God will be emphasised further.

The Master refers to the three great lights as 'the three great, though emblematical lights' in Freemasonry. So, for the aspirant, they will work as emblems, symbols, in which allegory will assist him in realising their power. The sacred writings are to govern his faith. Attending to God's will may mean for him

> **To explore:**
>
> • Figurative darkness in life
> • Selfish impulses
> • Ways of approaching light
> • Outer light – inner light
> • Symbols illuminate
> • The sacred volume
> • The square – constraining or liberating?
> • The compasses – retaining or releasing?

maintaining a true, straight path, a path to which he will always return if, in the future, he should find himself diverted from the pursuit of knowledge and light. The square is to regulate his actions, and is a symbol of the morality to which he aspires, leaving behind the old, base Self, to approach a higher plane. Square conduct implies adhering to a line of correctness in his dealings. The compasses are to keep him in due bounds with all mankind, therefore never overstepping the bounds of truth, moral conduct and propriety.

# 24 Three to Light Us

*Body, Soul, Spirit*

'You are now enabled to discover the three lesser lights. They are situated east, south and west, and are meant to represent the sun, moon and Master of the lodge…'

*After the aspirant has been restored to light in the first degree*

The three lesser lights are represented in lodges by pillars of the Ionic order at the Master's pedestal in the east, the Doric order at the Senior Warden's pedestal in the west, and the Corinthian order at that of the Junior Warden in the south.

The Master is placed in the east. In the same way that the sun diffuses light and lustre to all within its circle, and is indeed the source of life for all mankind, the aspirant may come to look on the Master as that medium through which light and instruction are communicated to the Brethren of the lodge. As God called the world into existence, in like manner the Master, and he alone in the lodge, has the power to call the lodge into existence, and to order it to be closed again at the end of labour, thereby raising the consciousness of those present at the opening, and gently lowering it at the closing. He is the source of spiritual light and guidance for all of the Brethren, but here especially for the aspirant on his journey. The Master, supremely in the lodge, represents the divine power, and no work can be achieved in a lodge without his presence.

The Senior Warden is placed in the west, the place of the setting sun, that place therefore emblematically depicted by the moon, the onset of night. He it is who pays the Brethren their wages at the end of a day of labour, conducting a reckoning with them, to reward labour but also to ensure that they pay their dues for any debts they may owe. His place is physically opposite the Master, and since he represents the onset of darkness and, ultimately, of the transformative aspect of the deity, he stands, in one sense, for the opposing agency to that of the Master. Death is God's way of transforming our nature at the end of our physical existence, an existence which began at the rising of our own sun in the east.

But the Senior Warden is also, with his junior partner, one of the two gatekeepers in the lodge, one of the two officers who interrogate aspirants on their pilgrimages as to their fitness to become Freemasons or to advance to a higher degree, a higher level of consciousness. As the Master represents the divine power, the spirit of man, so the Senior Warden represents one stage lower, the soul of man, not yet in contact with divinity. As the Master calls to labour, so the Senior Warden calls to rest at the end of the day.

The Junior Warden represents the human psyche, the Self, that part of man that existed before birth and will survive death, and stands for the journey between birth and death – the journey of life. He marks the position of the midday sun, and therefore the mid-point between the Master and the Senior Warden. Although it is the Master who represents the rising of the sun, it is the Junior Warden who represents its journey across the heavens and hence the course which our lives must run. As the Master calls the Brethren to labour and the Senior Warden calls them to rest at the end of labour, so the Junior Warden calls the Brethren to refreshment at midday. As one of the gatekeepers he also has charge of the admission of aspirants.

As we saw, the Master's position is denoted by the Ionic column, the emblem of wisdom. The Senior Warden's position is denoted by the Doric column, the emblem of strength, and the Junior Warden's by the Corinthian column, the emblem of beauty. The universe is the Temple of God, supported by three great pillars of these same names – wisdom, strength and beauty.

The lodge therefore, seen in the micro sense, is a model of man – psyche or Self (Junior Warden), soul (Senior Warden) and spirit, that which is in contact with the divinity (Master). But in the macro sense it is a model of the universe, the realm of heaven and earth combined, where wisdom conducts, strength fulfils and beauty enhances and enriches. And so it is with our definition of the lodge, for the lodge is said to be supported by three great pillars: wisdom, strength and beauty; wisdom to

**To explore:**

• Creation of the world, creation of the lodge
• Body – soul – spirit
• Paying wages – repaying debts
• Darkness transforms
• Birth – life – death
• Wisdom – strength – beauty
• Model of man – model of the universe
• The two Wardens

conduct us in all our undertakings, strength to support us under all our difficulties, and beauty to adorn the inward man. The inward man is important in all Freemasonry, since at our centre, our heart, is where the work is done and where the truth is to be found.

# 25 Enlightenment
## *Third degree audiences only*

*Light to illumine the path*

We often encounter darkness in life. Light is provided in Freemasonry to counter darkness.

We begin our life in the darkness of the womb. We end it in the darkness of the tomb. Between those two extremities, light is essential to our progress, in a literal, physical sense as well as in a figurative, symbolic sense. Of all the organs of sense with which humans have been equipped, the eyes are the most perceptive. Deprived of light, we are more helpless than when deprived of any other sense.

But deprived of spiritual light we can be yet more disabled, and we may have sought spiritual progress in Freemasonry because our own inner light was weak. When we set out on our Masonic journey, we were told that we would be deprived of light, so that did not come as a surprise to us. The reason for this deprivation only became clear, however, once we were under way. We were not to take notice of light from outside, nor to take notice of any outside influences, so that we could better concentrate on what was happening inside, so that we could identify and appreciate the inner light. This was a light which was faint at first, growing stronger as we felt our spirit grow stronger.

In the lodge of Entered Apprentices in which we were initiated, light was withheld only from us, not from the other members of the lodge. This was because the journey was ours alone, the journey away from the darkness of un-knowing to the light of knowledge of our Self. The other members of the lodge were there to help us on the journey, but they could not take part, since the journey was ours alone, the journey towards self-knowledge.

We may often think that we know ourselves, but this may be an illusion. If we regard ourselves in a mirror, do we believe that we see the true image, the true person as he or she is? Of course we do not. We see something very close to the real person, but we do not see ourselves as others see us, because the mirror has transposed our features – the left side has become the right, and vice versa. So it is clear that we will have to go deeper than skin deep to investigate the real Self, with its virtues and vices, strengths and failings.

Our restoration to material light later, followed the question 'Having been kept for a considerable time in a state of darkness, what is the predominant wish of your heart?'. The considerable time referred to here is not merely the time that has elapsed since we were admitted to the temple – it refers to the time, perhaps since birth, that we have spent wishing for more light for our heart, our spirit. It refers to the considerable time most of us spend in darkness, removed from spiritual riches, and therefore in poverty.

In the second degree, we ascended the winding staircase. Physically this brought us nearer to the sun. It also brought us nearer to the middle chamber, where we would become acquainted with the name of God, and therefore brought us nearer to that spiritual light that we sought. We were proceeding away from our base Self, with all its impulses and vices, towards our enlightened, purified Self, referred to in this degree by Joshua praying to God to continue the light of day, 'that he might complete the overthrow of his enemies', in other words that he might conquer the evil in himself.

In the third degree we encountered, not the personal darkness experienced by the aspirant in the first degree, but a general darkness experienced by all the members of the lodge. Through the lessons taught by the first and second degrees, and above all now that we had been admitted to the middle chamber, we were spiritually stronger, better equipped to withstand the severe trial of the third degree.

So here we figuratively faced death, and were deprived of all those supports which had so far accompanied us on our journey. The darkness here was far more profound, and needed a far greater light to penetrate it. Here we could indeed speak of divine light, the knowledge of God and the willingness, the eagerness, to adhere to the moral law, to reach greater heights of spiritual progress than heretofore. And this was made possible by piercing 'that mysterious veil which the eye of human *reason* cannot penetrate', namely that veil, constructed perhaps by ourselves, separating us from true knowledge of God, and therefore making it impossible for us to be one with our vital and immortal principle, the one-ness with God whereby we become whole and healthy, spiritually as well as physically.

**To explore:**

- When is light needed, when not
- Material light – spiritual light
- Personal darkness – general darkness
- Your own experience of darkness in your life
- Your own experience of light in your life
- How to see yourself, a mirror not being enough
- Veils separating us from truth – how they come about
- Why human understanding, reason, is not enough

## 26 Aspects of Freedom

*From servitude to new freedom*

'Mr Smith as no person can be made a Mason unless he is free and of mature age, I demand of you, are you a free man and of the full age of twenty-one years?'

*The Master's first words to the aspirant in the first degree*

Freedom. We are called Free Masons. What could that mean? You will find many Masonic meanings attributed to that word. One version has it that slaves could not be initiated. One field of research asserts that the operative stonemasons worked in free-stone, that is, limestone or sandstone, which had the characteristic of lending itself to Masonry and sculpting.

No doubt these allusions to freedom are valid for the aspirant. But surely the reference to freedom at this point in the initiation ceremony has more to it than these. Are we referring perhaps to physical freedom? Surely not, since the aspirant is, in a large sense, deprived of that very quality, being blindfolded and deprived of so much materially. He is led round almost as a slave might have been, unable to control the direction or speed of his progress, since these are determined by the Brother who conducted him.

Freedom for the aspirant of course does not consist in doing as he pleases, nor does it consist in giving full rein to all his impulses, greed, passions and desires. In fact he could say that those impulses enslave him, constrict him, limit his ability to think and act on the broad plane. If he is obsessed with the need to satisfy his appetites, enslaved by them, and he is offered the choice of following another, clearly-defined path, a route leading away from that obsession, even though it means adhering to some rules, then that can give him freedom, liberating him from his base Self, leading him out onto a bright, sunlit plain of rightness and harmony.

To choose freely to set out on a path where there are rules to guide and keep the aspirant, requires that he puts his trust in those who guide him. On entering the temple he gives up physical freedom. He gives up the ability to determine his own destiny. The Brethren in the temple have already placed a degree of trust in him, that he will prove to be worthy of the privilege of initiation. So too the aspirant places trust in the Brethren, that they will behave correctly towards him, and not abuse his trust in any way.

This is not the blind faith sometimes associated with religious zeal. It is the true spirit of enquiry, of an open, free heart, ready to learn, ready to exercise some of the aspirant's own insights. It is the ability to say: 'I free myself from my material and selfish concerns, in order to dedicate myself to pursuits that do not necessarily bring me material advantage.' This requires also that the aspirant frees himself from emotional burdens, as well as those of an ideological, social or sectarian nature. In short, it is the freedom of the open heart, the place where he is first prepared to be made a Freemason.

Look at the several allegorical ways in which the aspirant's freedom of action is constrained. The first, and perhaps the most powerful, is the one we have already mentioned: the blindfold. It is important that removing the faculty of sight is meant to hinder, for a time, the aspirant's onward physical progress. Then we have disarranged his clothing in such a way that he would be reluctant to venture out into the open. One shoe has been removed, making it difficult to walk properly. His money and valuables have been taken from him. A cable-tow has been placed round his neck as a symbol of submission. And a Brother holds him firmly by the hand, so that he no longer determines his own course forward. He can no longer outwardly say 'For man is man, and master of his fate.' He is told what to do, where to go, how to stand, how to move, how to behave, and he cannot even see where he is going, when and where to turn, what obstacles to avoid.

All of this is an allegory of the aspirant being obliged to trim himself, his actions and his impulses, to concentrate his mind away from material concerns, so that he may adjust to the imposition of a rule of life. This is a rule intended to speak to his heart and to tell him that so much of what he has given up may be of little worth, of little consequence. By giving up such things he may set out on a path of moral progress, of inner enlightenment.

---

**To explore:**

- Your own thoughts on what freedom can mean
- Whether freedom gives us licence to behave in any way we choose
- Trust
- How to enslave, how to liberate
- Freedom from burdens
- Rules – constraining or liberating?
- Impulses and appetites
- Deprivation of freedom – how it can be constraining, how liberating

---

# 27 Divine Wisdom

*Wisdom and beauty*

'Wisdom to conduct us in all our undertakings, strength to support us under all our difficulties, and beauty to adorn the inward man.'

*Part of the first lecture*

Wisdom is an elusive quality or characteristic. The dictionary refers to wisdom as the 'capacity of judging rightly in matters relating to life and conduct', and in other languages we have other aspects, other insights. In French, the word is *sagesse*, bearing undertones of sagacity. In German, *Weisheit* can also be rendered as 'knowingness'. This is not the same as 'knowledge', or learning a lot of facts, by reading and by other means.

Wisdom is more than this; wisdom is the condition in which the aspirant *knows*, sometimes through contemplation, the rightness of something, or its character. Judging rightly. But since he may have an idea of 'right' that differs from another person's, he needs an absolute right, namely that provided by God. In the prayer at initiation, we pray that the aspirant for Freemasonry may be endued with competency in, or become proficient in, the wisdom of God, absolute wisdom. If he clothes himself in this at the outset, he may, assisted by the Masonic journey, be able to unfold the beauties of godliness.

Here are three important words: 'godliness', 'beauties' and 'unfold'. Godliness is a hint of the aspirant's *other* nature, a nature beyond, his material nature. It refers him to a spirituality residing in each one of us which, once revealed, makes him one with God. The hermetic concept of 'as above, so below' teaches that the God or Gods of the ancients, perceived as a God in heaven above, or a God 'out there', is reflected, in a macro/micro sense, in a divinity residing in each one of us. By this doctrine, the supernatural is not merely a non-material world or sphere outside of ourselves to which our physical beings have no access, but rather it becomes intimately related to us, and allows of a concept of a divinity within ourselves, matching the God whom we worship and revere, and whose laws we obey, since those laws are the laws of universal morality.

Such godliness is enshrined in, and forms a part of, the beauty in the creation, so that by discovering, or remembering, those parts of himself where ugliness and discord have no place, the aspirant is enabled, or empowered, to focus on the positive aspects of his inner Self.

The world seems sometimes to be full of strife and discord. Loud and strident voices are to be heard everywhere proclaiming the 'rightness' of some particular position, the 'wrongness' of those who do not agree. What we might wish for the aspirant here is to acknowledge that degree of 'rightness' which he may, by contemplation, discover in himself. By this means, he may recognise where the beauty of harmony resides. For it is the search for, and promotion of, beauty to which he may be dedicated. The quality of beauty is often misunderstood. Visual, sensual beauty of course is one thing, but inner, figurative, non-sensual beauty is that which deserves the aspirant's attention. Later, he will study virtue, that quality described in the lecture as 'the integrity, harmony and just balance of affection; the health, strength and beauty of the soul'. For the aspirant, the beauties of true godliness begin to take on a special meaning.

But 'unfold' is the key to the whole phrase. Godliness, and the beauty that attends it, are not to be searched for outside, or obtained simply by rigorous religious observance. The aspirant will get nowhere if he searches for this in the world outside. It resides in himself, and this key word, 'unfold', tells him that he can attain to godliness by the active work necessary to bring it forth, something that has always been a part of him. The competency, proficiency in God's wisdom, is the divine aid he seeks, and which the Master seeks on his behalf in reciting the prayer.

Later, the aspirant will learn that the three great pillars supporting a Freemason's lodge are wisdom, strength and beauty. Here, he has two of them to which to apply some insight: wisdom and beauty. The spiritual strength is yet to come.

---

**To explore:**

• What you understand by wisdom
• Some ideas of unfolding goodness from within yourself
• Our relationship with God
• God outside, God inside ourselves
• From discord to harmony
• Harmony as a component of beauty
• Outer beauty, inner beauty

---

# 28 Unfolding Godliness

*Divinity in ourselves*

'Endue him with a competency of Thy divine wisdom that, assisted by the secrets of our Masonic art, he may the better be enabled to unfold the beauties of true godliness...'

*From the prayer in the first degree*

When the Master says the words of this prayer, he recognises that the aspirant is in need of initiation as a route away from his base Self, rising to a fuller, brighter existence, a real moral and ethical improvement in himself, a journey towards God. He gives recognition to the fact that the aspirant is in need of wisdom, and which of us is not?

The words of this prayer, however, conceal something of supreme importance for Freemasons: 'he may the better be enabled to unfold the beauties of true godliness'. We first have to ask ourselves: how am I to unfold the promised godliness? Then we have to ask: and where is it situated?

One explanation of this is as follows. Quests for an explanation of non-material phenomena have existed since the beginning of the human race. In the ancient world, these quests came to belong to a general body of thought referred to as the Mysteries. The core of the Mysteries was that there existed two parallel worlds, both of which we inhabit at the same time. There was the physical, material, sensual world – a world with edges – and there were the vast, limitless, eternal, non-material realms, not limited by physical phenomena, and not available to ordinary perception, but which were still a part of our universe.

In these realms, the arenas for the exploits of the gods of mythology, events occurred which were governed by the same natural laws existing in our world of ordinary experience, events which had an important influence on the daily activity of human life. The closest of these non-material domains exists in our own psyche, since every time we dream, we are participants in such supernatural events, the boundary of the inaccessible part of that domain being the threshold of our own consciousness.

The Mysteries were schools which provided the gateway to those non-material realms, and to the knowledge of the natural laws operating in them. They existed for the satisfaction of those who wished to know more, those who wished to understand divinity, directly, for themselves. How did they do this? Incorporated in the practice of the ancient Mysteries was a process of initiation, a process directly comparable with Masonic initiation.

In those ancient times, from those realms where the writers of our ritual very probably took their inspiration, in the philosophy of the Greek god Hermes was formulated the idea 'as above, so below' as an induction into explaining the universe. The full saying is, 'That which is above is like that which is below, and that which is below is like that which is above, to achieve the wonders of the One.' This encapsulates the idea that the universe is the same as God; God is the same as man; man is the same as the cell; the cell is the same as the atom, and so on. To sum it up, this message theorises that man is the counterpart of God on earth, just as God is man's counterpart in life eternal. Therefore it is a statement of an ancient belief that man's actions on earth mirror the actions of God in life eternal.

This concept is represented in Freemasonry by two important symbols. The hexalpha is a six-pointed star formed by inverting one triangle over another, and interlacing them in such a way that one point is directed towards heaven, and the other towards earth, pointing out how man's nature is inextricably that of God. Jacob's ladder similarly illustrates that earth and heaven are connected, with angels both ascending and descending on it.

This is a long way of saying that if man's consciousness is brought to bear on his own nature, he may discover that element within himself which is divine. We often call our own or others' gifts 'God-given', meaning that without divine aid, our own efforts are worthless. One of the psalms in the Old Testament says, 'Except the Lord build the house, they labour in vain that build it: except the Lord keep the city, the watchman waketh but in vain.' By our own heightened state of consciousness

**To explore:**

• Unfolding virtues
• Humanity and godliness
• Material and non-material existences
• Connections between earth and heaven
• Building relying on our own strength only
• Building relying on our own strength aided by God
• The nature of wisdom

in the first degree lodge, we may arrive at that state where our own nature approaches that of God. We may be able to build better through self-knowledge, that is, knowledge of a potential in ourselves that we may never have realised, a potential that reflects the divine spark which resides in us all.

Freemasonry, we are told, teaches moral lessons and self-knowledge. If we invert this statement, then self-knowledge becomes a route to moral progress. If, as suggested above, self-knowledge begins by acknowledging that divine spark within us, we will through that acknowledging ultimately increase also in wisdom, the first of the three pillars supporting a Freemason's temple. Wisdom may be regarded as an understanding of the highest principles of things, that functions as a guide for living a truly exemplary life. We have all known people whom we regard as wise by that definition, but we probably have little idea of how to achieve wisdom for ourselves.

But this is no ordinary wisdom. The wisdom promised by this prayer is divine wisdom, the wisdom of an eternal and omnipotent Being, and by the principle of 'as above, so below' we may come in time to understand much more than our upbringing or our education has taught us.

# 29 Compasses
## *Third degree audiences only*

*Freedom and limitations*

The compasses form one of the three great lights, one of the working tools in the third degree, and an implement made use of in other parts of all three degrees.

The compasses are an implement met with many times in Freemasonry. The first time, in initiation, is when the aspirant holds the compasses in his left hand, one point presented to his heart, for the heart is the centre of his being; it is in his heart that he is first prepared to be made a Mason; and an open heart, a heart that is free, is the first and most important pre-condition of membership.

When it is said that the heart is where a man is first prepared to be made a Mason, we mean that it is to his intuition, his instinct for what is right, that Freemasonry appeals. He is not using what we commonly understand by intellect. He will not be attracted to Freemasonry by the intellect of the mind. He will not wish to join because of some pursuit of academic endeavour. His motives will have more to do with where and how he sees himself, or perhaps because his attempts to know himself up to now have not been fruitful.

The aspirant is blindfolded. He hears the words of the Master and the other officers, but he is unable to discern the nature of the objects around him. At the door he is asked 'Do you feel anything?' but he is unable to tell what it is that he feels. By contrast, when he kneels to make his vow, the Master tells him explicitly that he is placing his right hand on the Volume of the Sacred Law, and that his left hand will be employed in supporting the compasses, so for the first time he is aware of the nature of two of the objects in the lodge: the Sacred Volume and the compasses.

After his blindfold is removed, before the aspirant's attention can be distracted, the Master points out to him the three great, though emblematical, lights in Freemasonry – the Volume of the Sacred Law, the square and compasses. The compasses keep him in due bounds with all mankind, particularly his Brethren in Freemasonry. They are therefore an implement with which he can measure out how far from the centre to proceed, without exceeding the limits of propriety, or moral conduct.

So it is from the centre that he proceeds. One point of the compasses denotes the centre: the other describes the circumference. Depicted on the tracing board in the first degree is a circle between two parallel lines. The lecture says, 'In all regular, well-formed, constituted lodges there is a point within a circle round which the Brethren cannot err; this circle is bounded between north and south by two parallel lines, one representing Moses, the other King Solomon.' On top of the circle rests the Sacred Volume, supporting Jacob's ladder. In going round this circle Freemasons touch on both of the parallel lines and also on the Sacred Volume, and keeping themselves circumscribed in this way, they cannot err.

In another essay we speak of freedom, and the way it differs from licence. Licence is doing as we like, as much as we like. Freedom, however, is different. It denotes our freedom of inclination and freedom of intent, but it is personal to us and does not imply lack of limits. This aspect of limits to our actions is a crucial aspect of the compasses as a Masonic emblem. In the lecture, referring to the third of the immovable jewels of the lodge, we are reminded that the perfect ashlar is 'a stone of a true die or square', representing a life led according to moral precepts which 'can no otherwise be tried and approved than by the square of God's word and the compass of his own self-convincing conscience'. So the compasses are there to measure such actions in life, and our own conscience will be our best guide. 'To keep us in due bounds with all mankind' therefore must mean that our freedom allows us, requires us, to act to the limit of our faculties and the best of our abilities, but not to such an extent that it affects the freedom of those around us.

The compasses become more important still in the third degree. Here, the working tools are the skirret, pencil and compasses. Here the third of the three great lights is given to the aspirant to work with. The compasses, we are told, define the limits of good and evil. By adhering to the centre, where the first leg of the compasses is placed, the aspirant adheres to the moral law. To stray over the limit set by the other leg of the compasses is to disregard the moral law, that code by which we live in harmony with our fellow-men. In the words of the first degree, while the aspirant keeps himself thus circumscribed, he cannot err.

**To explore:**

- The first point of the compasses indicates the heart, the centre
- An instinct for what is right
- Intellect of the mind – of the heart
- How far from the centre to proceed
- Fixing limits
- Where is the centre – where the circumference?
- Freedom inside the circle – licence outside it
- The compass of your conscience

# 30 Peace
## *Second and third degree audiences only*

*Back to the centre again*

'Before we open the lodge in the second degree, let us supplicate the Grand Geometrician of the Universe, that the rays of heaven may shed their influence to enlighten us in the paths of virtue and science.'

*Prayer in the second degree opening*

'In this position, what have you discovered?'

'A sacred symbol.'

'Where is it situated?'

'In the centre of the building.'

'To whom does it allude?'

'The Grand Geometrician of the Universe.'

*Closing the second degree lodge*

What is the great lesson of the second degree? Is it Joshua fighting the battles of the Lord, or Jephtha beating off his enemies? It is more likely that the greatest lesson here has more to do with peaceable pursuits than with warlike ones.

The second degree is a degree of journeying, the degree of life. It has not the dramatic sudden allegory of the enlightenment of the first degree. It has not the intense drama and the blinding revelation of the third. It is a restful degree, a degree of retrospection, recollection and peace. The temple and the general form of the lodge opening and of the ceremony present us with a more or less familiar landscape through which to make our way, slowly, meditatively, as we learn – but learn we must, in order to progress through it.

In order to learn, we need light with which to see, so that we can interpret this new symbolism in our hearts. To start with, we will need God's light, the rays of heaven referred to in the opening, since symbols, although discerned by the eye, need to imprint themselves on a deeper level than the visual. We are enjoined, in this degree, to 'contemplate the intellectual faculty'. What does that mean? Here we deal not with the supposed intellect of the mind, of book knowledge or academic learning. This is an intellect of the heart, of intuition and feeling, so easy to immerse ourselves in, so rewarding, but so challenging also, since now it is with our hearts that we must learn, or remember.

'The secrets of nature, and the principles of intellectual truth' are where we are headed. Nature of course refers us to our own nature – by knowing ourselves, we may reach 'intellectual truth', to understand our own heart and thereby our relation to our fellowmen and the world around us. These then are *real* secrets, secrets of great importance to each one of us. And they are concealed because it is only in revealing them to ourselves, each one of us, that they begin to have some value.

So it is also with nature and science. They are mysteries, because we must not contemplate them only on a superficial level; we have to trace them down to their deepest imports. They are *hidden* mysteries, because we must come to realise that there is more to them than meets the eye. Who am I? We may look in a mirror and see an image, but that image as we know has been transposed, so that the left hand is now the right hand and vice versa. We are looking at a likeness, but it is not the real person, a person whom we *think* we know, but may be surprised when we dig deep.

To complete the quotation above from the second degree ritual: 'to contemplate the intellectual faculty and to trace it from its development, through the paths of heavenly science, even to the throne of God Himself'. Where were we first prepared to be made a Mason? In our heart. This is where the intellectual faculty resides, which, in the first degree, we hope to develop by moral progress. Knowledge of ourselves follows; heavenly science is the path we tread, leading

**To explore:**

• Your own ideas of peace, stillness
• Learning with the mind, with the heart
• The heart – feeling and knowing
• Nature and truth
• Concealing and revealing
• Images in a mirror, in life
• Paths of heavenly science
• Your own idea of the centre

us, in the second degree, to the door of the middle chamber. Then, once qualified, we are led into the middle chamber itself, where we come to know more of God, and begin to realise that God is at the centre, not some abstract centre, some indistinct point somewhere in the universe, but at our own centre.

And this brings us full circle, in more senses than one, back to the first degree and the lecture there:

'In all regular, well-formed, constituted lodges there is a point within a circle round which the Brethren cannot err; this circle is bounded between north and south by two grand parallel lines, one representing Moses, the other King Solomon; on the upper part of this circle rests the Volume of the Sacred Law, supporting Jacob's ladder... In going round this circle we must necessarily touch on both those parallel lines, likewise on the Sacred Volume, and while a Mason keeps himself thus circumscribed, he cannot err.'

At the centre, truly found, is peace.

# Index

# T

# UV

# W